Shotokan Karate
KATA Vol. 1

Joachim Grupp

SHOTOKAN KARATE
KATA VOL. 1

Meyer & Meyer Sport

Original title: Shotokan Karate Kata 1
© Aachen: Meyer & Meyer, 2000

Shotokan Karate Kata Vol. 1
British Library Cataloguing in Publication Data
A catalogue record for this book is available from the British Library

Shotokan Karate Kata Vol. 1
Joachim Grupp
Maidenhead: Meyer & Meyer Sport (UK) Ltd., 2003
ISBN: 978-1-84126-282-6

© 2003 by Meyer & Meyer Sport (UK) Ltd.
2nd, revised edition 2009
Aachen, Adelaide, Auckland, Budapest, Cape Town, Graz, Indianapolis,
Maidenhead, Olten (CH), Singapore, Toronto
Member of the World
Sport Publishers' Association (WSPA)
www.w-s-p-a.org
Printed by: B.O.S.S Druck und Medien GmbH
ISBN: 978-1-84126-282-6
E-Mail: info@m-m-sports.com
www.m-m-sports.com

Contents

Foreword

What are Kata, and what is the purpose of this book? As a traditional, set form of techniques used against more than one attackers, Kata are the essential elements of Karate. Prior to the introduction of Kumite – exercises with a partner – Kata were practically the only things used for practice. All today's elements of Karate stem from the Kata. The fascination of the Kata opens the way for everyone with sufficient patience to continually practice their techniques and sequences and continually improve their execution. This book should contribute to supporting these aims and assist the Karateka in perfecting his prowess in the Kata, whether it is in order to pass gradings, for daily training, for working on oneself, for Karate-Do or for competitions. A such, the book constitutes only one way to be helped. It can be used to complement training in a dojo or club, but it cannot replace it. Correct breathing, tensing the muscles and relaxing them, the interchange between rapid and slow movements, timing and many other aspects can only be learned through intensive training.

Kata is one of the three pillars of Karate. Alongside Kihon and Kumite, Kata training is an important aspect of Karate exercises today. Without continuous practice of the Kata skills, Karate-Do would be unthinkable. They include: a myriad of techniques, which are seldom or not at all practised in Kumite or basic training; techniques for close combat; grips or sequences to start throws; defence against armed aggressors; and attacks against sensitive body areas, all of which cannot be trained for without endangering a sparring partner. Indeed, the range of techniques contained in the Kata is almost inexhaustible.

A further aspect should not go unmentioned – the aesthetics. It is simply fun to practice the Kata or to watch a demonstration of Kata. To the observer, Kata have the effect of a particular kind of fascination, more than perhaps in the other aspects of Karate. The aesthetics of an excellently performed Kata in training or in competition cannot simply be ignored. It is quite noticeable how much energy is expressed in this form of fighting against an imaginary opponent. Tension, speed, precision, dynamics, power and explosiveness in the techniques – a good Kata demonstration brings all of Karate's many aspects to the fore.

The special characteristics of a particular style are reflected in the Kata. In Shotokan Karate, there is a large spectrum of different Kata. While the focus of the Kata in our style lies mainly more in dynamic, rapid and explosive movements, the 26 Kata in Shotokan are nevertheless divided into two categories: those that tend to be more rapid and explosive in the Shorin tradition, and those that concentrate on the breathing and power side of the Shorin tradition. The Shorin group includes the Heian Katas, Empi, Bassai-Dai, Kanku-Dai, Nijushiho and the Gojushiho Kata. They also concentrate on the breathing techniques and consist of rather slower sequences; but the basic tempo is rapid and dynamic. Those that concentrate more on power are in the Shorei group, e.g., Jion and Hangetsu as well as Sochin and Jitte.

This book contains the basic Kata up to Tekki 1, and the initial Master Kata Bassai-Dai.

When training in the Kata, one main principle must not be forgotten: training in a particular Kata should not exceed the technical capability of the individual. In all cases, a Kata in a lower category perfected well is hugely preferable to a badly executed Kata in a higher category. Therefore, the Heian Kata should first be practised intensively before you go on to learn the next Kata group. Thus, the learning and practising of an individual Kata will be correspondingly longer, and you should not refrain from practising Kata that you already think you can do over and over again. You never master a Kata perfectly. You are always in the process of doing this.

A description of the basic techniques for Shotokan Karate is not included in this book. If you are practising Kata, you should already have some idea of the basics. At this point, I would like to draw your attention to my book "Shotokan Karate. Kihon, Kumite, Kata" (2nd edition, Maidenhead 2009), which contains this information.

I wish all readers who want to practice and come to terms with the fascination of Shotokan Kata lots of fun in reading the lessons here, and good luck with Karate-Do.

1 INTRODUCTION

1.1 The History of Shotokan Karate

"Karate-Do is achieved a step at a time, just like life. Just train every day and do your best and the truth will come to you." (Masatoshi Nakayama)

The origins of Karate lie in Okinawa. Several hundred kilometres away from the Japanese mainland is the island whose inhabitants developed fighting techniques centuries ago that they used to defend themselves from invaders and armed aggressors. Through healthy trade connections and cultural exchanges with other neighbouring Asian countries, a heterogeneous martial art emerged out of the already existing local weapon and fighting techniques. The economic centres of Shuri, Naha and Tomari were the focus of this development.

The development of martial arts on Okinawa received a large impetus as far back as 1429 after the ban on weapons was decreed by King Sho Shin. Before even the Chinese influence of Chuan-Fa had gained a foothold on the island, the martial art of Te (Te = hand) was being taught by several masters. This occurred, however, in small schools and closed circles. It cannot be assumed that this martial art was standardised or, from today's standpoint, that it was a fully developed art.

In 1372, in the vicinity of Naha, several Chinese families settled and brought Buddhism with them. It is assumed that they had an influence on Te throughout the area of Naha. It is held that the local popular Naha-Te (later called Shorei-Ryu – 'Ryu' means 'school') was inspired from the traditions of Chuan-Fa. It consists of dynamic movements and puts value on breathing and the technique for producing rapid and explosive power. The interest in Chinese culture amongst the Okinawans was large and, as a result, the philosophy and the fighting techniques of Chinese boxing (Kempo) spread into several regions of Okinawa. Other centres for Te were Tomari and Shuri (the styles developed here were later also called Shorin-Ryu). A Chinese influence could also be found in Shuri-Te, with its emphasis on breathing control and round defensive movements. Tomari-Te contains, on the other hand, both these elements.

The inhabitants of Okinawa lived mainly as farmers, fishermen or traders. Very often the specific characteristics of the old style can be related to the different traditions of their professions. The American historian Randall HASSELL sees various social traditions as the roots of the different martial-art systems: The farming community preferred a style with a low stance posture so that they could defend themselves with both arms and the legs from low positions. HASSELL traces another powerful style with numerous arm movements to the fishermen.

The farmers and the fishermen were also inventive in using their work implements as weapons. Kobudo, the use of a Bo, the Tonfa, Nunchaka Kama and other tools used as weapons comes from this epoch. Today's Kata still contain, in part, (defensive) movements against such weapons.

The Japanese occupied Okinawa in 1609 and subjugated its inhabitants. This led to a ban on Te under the Satsuma dynasty at the time of Iesha Shimazu. As a result, could only be practised in secrecy. Nevertheless, there were several masters who were deeply respected and taught their art further in secret. The fighting techniques were intertwined as a sort of code into the Kata. Training was also done using the Makiwara, where techniques could be executed with lots of energy and power. The need to be able to defeat an armed aggressor using a decisive technique – and even to kill him – was expressed in the whole system of training. This concentrated and focussed on vital points of the body and played an important role.

The masters of this art were well-respected in the community, but they did not consider themselves almighty. It is therefore futile to philosophically glorify the beginnings back in the dark ages of this martial art or to try to justify the origins historically. Missing written evidence makes any statement in this way merely speculative. It is, however, a fact that the fighting system created by the fishermen and farmers of Okinawa served one purpose above all: to be able to kill an enemy who was superior both in weaponry and equipment in order to survive.

The reforms of the Meiji government, which superseded the Satsuma reign in 1868, permitted the development of martial arts and their popularity throughout the whole country.

In those days, the basic martial art that we know as Karate was called "Okinawa-Te" or "Tang-Te". The latter of these two descriptions ("Tang" means Chinese) expressed the high respect held for anything coming from China. Te, as it was then, is not yet considered by historians to be a complete or even standardised martial art. Completely differing styles had been developed in the various areas. Some consisted of very few techniques that had been practised for years and years. Some masters of the art even possessed a very limited repertoire. Some sources report that they practised only one-to-three techniques for the whole of their lives, but these were carried out to perfection.

Historian Robin L REILLY, who has conducted comprehensive research into the history of Karate, tells us that, following its liberalisation in the 19th Century, large rivalries developed amongst the Te schools (Shuri, Naha and Tomari). Very often this turned into open conflicts between the adherents, which had a negative effect on the high reputation of the Te martial art at that time.

This all changed when Te became a sport in the school curriculum. The young Master Gichin FUNAKOSHI made a great impression on some civil servants when he gave a demonstration of his skills and showed off his excellent physical condition. Consequently, Te was introduced into the schools in Okinawa in 1902. Thus, the cornerstone was laid for a change in the martial art, which had started out as a mere method of survival and was fast becoming a type of popular sport. The reason, at that time, for the inclusion of Karate in the school curriculum is interesting: Karate was thougt of as being conducive to training the concentration and physical condition of pupils. The self-defence aspect was more in the background.

Gichin FUNAKOSHI, born in 1868, very quickly achieved great popularity and moved to Japan, where he stayed for the rest of his life developing modern Karate with great success. He was a student of the Masters AZATO and ITOSU and, using his great knowledge, he developed not only modern Karate but also the Shotokan style. He also 'Japanised' the original term "Tang", borrowed from the Chinese ("Tang-Te" means "Chinese hand"), and introduced the Japanese character and term, turning it into "Kara" ("Kara" means "empty"). This also happened as a reaction to the increasing self-awareness of the Japanese and their dissociation from Chinese influences. The term "Kara", however, equally includes the philosophical principles – the way to perfection of character and the unification of body and soul – that are integrated into this martial art.

In 1917, after FUNAKOSHI had demonstrated his style of martial art in Japan for the first time at the behest of the government, the impetus this gave to Karate knew no bounds. He pursued his aim – spreading the art of Karate – with inexhaustible zeal and this made him even more successful. This was not only because he was a highly educated master whose activities as a Karate instructor drew the attention of powerful individuals in government circles and the royal family. FUNAKOSHI also worked as a successful calligraphist and author, publishing his works under the nom de plume of "Shoto". He was well-known in Japan and more and more followers rallied round him, above all many from the intellectual milieu in universities and from military circles. His great popularity in the universities helped his Karate teaching later to reach worldwide popularity, as many of his pupils at the universities were destined to go abroad at a later point.

In Okinawa itself, several masters were against the change and the renaming of their martial art Te into Karate. They accused FUNAKOSHI of being a traitor to the traditions of Okinawa. This did no damage, however, to his success. Later on, many of these critics adopted the name of "Karate" for their own martial art.

In addition to the long tradition of the predominant Kata form of Karate training, in the 1930s, FUNAKOSHI developed training with a partner: Gohon Kumite, Kihon Ippon Kumite, Jiyu Ippon Kumite and free-fighting. He borrowed sequences from the Kata that were practised with a partner using various techniques. In this way a programme was created that came very close to self-defence. Kata training was now devoted more to the aim of achieving flexibility, speed and muscle strengthening. Aesthetic dimensions were also gradually being taken into account. The daily, routine practice of Karate in three elements that we know today as Kihon, Kumite and Kata came about at that time.

In 1939, FUNAKOSHI was already over 70 years old. In addition to his style – Shotokan Karate – further styles of Karate, such as Goju-Ryu, Shito-Ryu and Wado-Ryu, had been developed. These styles were also introduced by masters from Okinawa.

In honour of their master, FUNAKOSHI, several influential students built a dojo, which they named "Shotokan". This means "the hall of Shoto" and was from then on the term used for his style. The symbol for Shotokan Karate, the tiger in a circle, was designed by the famous artist Hoan KOSUGI, a friend of FUNAKOSHI, to illustrate his books about Karate. This is also the symbol widely used and adopted worldwide by Shotokan Karate clubs and associations even today.

Shortly after the end of the war, in 1949, the Japan Karate Association (JKA) was founded and, with it, the joint organisation of all the dojos, Karate groups and university schools in the whole of Japan that practised FUNAKOSHI's Shotokan style. The JKA became the association for all Shotokan Karateka in Japan and, later, worldwide. The other styles had also formed their own associations. The JKA organisation's symbol – called Inyo – remains the small dark circle in the larger empty circle right up to today. It represents the duality of the universe, and, like the Yin and Yan, it represents the oppsing forces in the universe.

The worldwide teaching of Shotokan is mainly based on the development of instructor prgrammes over many years at the Takushoku University. It was here in the 1950s, in a commercially and technically oriented university, that a very stiff and demanding education programme was held. Only the best Karate students could take part, and they were destined to assume instructor positions abroad at a later date. The programme of instruction was drawn up under the supervision of FUNAKOSHI by NAKAYAMA, OKAZAKI and NISHUAMA. These people held leading positions in the JKA and were responsible for the sporting aspects of the association's development. Together with FUNAKOSHI, they gave Karate demonstrations to many, including American soldiers on US Air Force bases. Later, the JKA sent 30 of its best instructors around the world in order to spread the teaching of Shotokan Karate. Amongst them were well-known Karate masters, such as KANAZAWA, KASE, SHIRAI, NISHIJAMA, OKAZAKI, MIKAMI, OKAMOTO, KAWAZOE, NAITO, OCHI, ENOEDA and many others remembered even today.

The high technical standards of the JKA and the development of the style stayed under FUNAKOSHI's direction as the Karate repertoire, the scholastic foundation of the Karate techniques and the introduction of competitive Karate were brought to their heights. Masatoshi NAKAYAMA inherited all this after FUNAKOSHI's death in 1957, and he was named as the highest official in the JKA. After his studies, he had lived in China for a long time and brought new techniques from there. Just as FUNAKOSHI would have done, he also studied the lesser-known styles and integrated the essentials into the Shotokan system, e.g., the original Goju-Ryu Kata Hangetsu. In the 1930s, NAKAYAMA had already taken on the task of learning the Gojushiho Kata and Nijushiho of the Master MABUNI and adapting them for the Shotokan style. Together with FUNAKOSHI and his son Giko, who had introduced the Sochin Kata, NAKAYAMA continued developing the system to create a unified martial art, and this soon included all the important elements. In Shotokan, there are not only the simple and rapid elements of the Shorin-Ryu, but also the powerful and emphasised breathing system of the Shorei-Ryu.

The instructors, and particularly NAKAYAMA, now published books laying out the basic principles that the style's techniques were scientifically based on.

At the same time, just like in other Budo disciplines, competition was introduced as an effective means of advertising the sport. By the 1950s, all the important Karate styles had adopted free-fighting, and the difficulty with this was the production of a system of rules like those that already existed for Judo, Kendo and other martial arts sports. The concept of carrying out competitions in Budo sports is not specific to Karate alone, and the idea was also not conceived by the JKA.

Judo, Kendo and other Budo arts were more advanced in this respect than Karate at that time. These martial arts had also successfully managed to integrate a sporting component into their system. In 20th-century Japan, it was no longer necessary to have to kill someone using the martial arts in order to survive, unlike life in the pre-Meiji regime of the 19th century. In addition, the sportsman should be protected against injury by a meaningful set of rules, without which they already had suffered for a long time during competitions.

After a five-year test phase, in 1956, the JKA came out with its first rule book and, in 1957, the first All-Japan Masters Championship was held. The difficulty in defining the competition rules that the organising instructors, NISHIJAMA, NAKAYAMA and others ran up against led them to ban many dangerous techniques from matches that were impossible or almost impossible to control. Still, the secret was to stay as far as possible within the traditions of the Karate-Do. In addition to Kumite competitions, the JKA instructors also created rules for the Kata discipline.

The concept of competition being included in the repertoire of JKA Shotokan Karate remained under the leadership of FUNAKOSHI, who headed the JKA until his death in 1957. The father of modern Karate knew that this aspect was also important in order to guarantee the longevity of Karate as a martial art in Japan alongside the other Budo disciplines.

However, he was still critical about these developments. FUNAKOSHI was not particularly conservative in his handling of Karate. For the whole of his life, he was only interested in spreading his style. To do this he had already brought in many innovations, reforms and breaks with the Okinawan tradition in order to perfect his system. He had already adapted Karate in 1902 from the original idea of the "art of killing in order to survive" to being a school sport. He had changed the names of the Kata and 'Japanised' the term "Karate" and the names of the Kata – all much against the insistence of the Okinawan masters.

In order to create a unified martial arts system and to bring it to be accepted in Japan, the competition had to be one aspect amongst many. This is why the match bout represents the last building block in the development of the Shotokan system, particularly considering the difficulty of making it succeed in Japan. As he should have, though, FUNAKOSHI remained sceptical about an interpretation of Karate that was only based on the issue of success in sport. In an interview about FUNAKOSHI's standpoint on the introduction of competition, NAKAYAMA said:

"He was very concerned that, if competition became too popular, students would ignore the basic principles and only train for match bouts. He realised that there would be competitions and that they would be important for making Karate internationally popular. However, he also wanted to make it clear that the basic schooling and training must be the prime important point."

Since the JKA and those Karate associations that followed JKA traditions wanted to dispel these fears of FUNAKOSHI, they prioritized Kata and Kihon and saw the competition as merely a facet of the Karate-Do spectrum. This natural evolution in Karate can be compared with that of Judo. Master Funakoshi carried on living for the rest of his life in Japan. He made Karate into a systemised art with a scholastic undertone, similar to the way the Japanese scholar Jigoro Kano developed Jiu-Jitsu into Judo. He also made it possible that harmless fights could take place in the art of Karate.

As has been illustrated, the development of a sporting dimension in Karate is not due to a "westernisation" of Karate. On the contrary, it represented the social situation in Japan. Although Karate today is not thinkable without the "Shiai" – the sporting bout –, only a very small minority practise Karate also as a competitive sport. As a result, this aspect of Karate is only, in effect, a widening of the horizon belonging to those practising Karate. Whether it be Kata or Kumite, sporting success would not be possible in a Karate competition without a high degree of self-discipline and concentration. This is what lies behind the concept of "Ikken Hissatsu" – killing with a single blow – in the philosophy of the Ippon in competitions (maintaining the tradition of Karate-Do). In addition there is the aspect of discipline and respect for the opponent. Taking part in competitions is the whetstone on which razor sharpness in Karate is honed.

With realistic situations and fair rules and conditions, this makes it possible for the Karateka to study the effectiveness of his techniques or his mental preparation. In point of fact, all of the great Japanese and western Karate masters have a successful period as competitors behind them. However, after having spent a short part of his life participating in competitions, the Karateka should continue practising Karate-Do as a way of life.

In 1957, the year of the first Japanese Masters Championships, FUNAKOSHI died at the ripe old age of almost 90. According to reports by JKA instructor Teruyuki OKAZAKI, he was still giving instruction in the central dojo of the JKA every day right up to a few days before his death. The JKA continued with FUNAKOSHI's aim – the spreading of Shotokan Karate – with worldwide success under the leadership of Masatoshi NAKAYAMA.

The interpretation of Karate by the JKA is still today the model example for the majority of the estimated 4-5 million Karateka following the Shotokan style. When it comes to the interpretation of Karate, the JKA technical guidelines – and particularly those set by NAKAYAMA – have continued to be authoritative throughout the world even today.

Today it is generally recognised that the wealth of traditional Karate-Do lies particularly in the fact that it fulfils a variety of demands; whether it is Karate as a popular sport practised to maintain the health in all age groups, as a martial art for self-defence, as a way to the inner-self or as a competitive sport. The reasons for practising the martial art Karate-Do are as varied as the mentality and makeup of the people who practise it.

Above all, however, it is respect and courtesy for others that should be paramount. The question of which is the 'correct' main area of Karate cannot be definitively answered. All facets of Karate-Do today can be interesting and valuable for the development and self-esteem of the individual. Which main area one will focus on depends on the person and the stage the person finds himself in his Karate career. Karate means different things to different people. It is, nevertheless, important to tolerate other conceptions of Karate, since Karate-Do offers an enormous variety of possibilities.

1.1.1 Karate-Do

The incorporation of Okinawa-Te into a school sport, its "export" worldwide and its transformation into a Japanese martial art brought the influence of Zen Buddhism into the equation more and more. The origins of Karate occurred in an era when it was a 'weapon' for the farmer and the fisherman. The origins had nothing to do with anything philosophical or even related to the Samurai. This spiritual and ethical influence had not yet played a part in the techniques of the Okinawan inhabitants. The problem for the farmer and the fisherman was one of survival. Only later, when the simple question of survival was no longer a necessity and when the Japanese martial arts and those from elsewhere began to influence things, did Karate begin to include strong philosophical elements.

In this respect, the term "Do" has a special meaning. In English, the word "Do" means "way". Just as with Karate, many other martial arts – including Judo, Kendo and Aikido – use the same term in conjunction with the main name of the art. In the 19th century, these Budo arts still had the word "Jutsu" (meaning 'technique') added. Kenjutsu and Karate-Jutsu were the "techniques with the sword" and the "techniques with the empty hand", respectively. The necessity of using techniques that are traced back to the idea of killing in self-defence lies behind this terminology. Late 19th-century Japan saw this necessity no longer existing. In numerous Kenjutsu schools at that time, competitions using the bamboo sword – "Shinai" – took place, and these quickly became popular, leading to the of the name "Kendo". The changeover from the original term "sword technique" to "way of the sword" was determined by the new social circumstances in which these arts, which were handed down from the Samurai, were now practised.

"Do" describes the way to mastering the art. This is the long 'road' that should bring about improvement in character and technical skills by not only having the aim of mastering the discipline, but also by working on the psychological and physical attributes of the sportsman's personality. Continuous work on oneself is the way and not the vision of the end product.

Zen Buddhism had been spreading in Japan since the Kamakura period (1185-1333). It can be traced back to the Indian monk BODHIDHARMA, and it found its supporters amongst the Samurai. He taught that inspiration (Satori) could only be achieved by intense physical and mental meditation. Only by closely sticking to these forms of meditation can one transcend from (logical) thought to an openness and harmony between body and spirit.

Obedience and the voluntary subjugation of the student to the guidance of the Zen master were the main elements of this religion. One can see here parallels in the relationships between the Samurai and their feudal lords. In their code of conduct, called "Bushido", they swore themselves to strict loyalty to the upperclass. Their obedience went as far as ritual suicide with a sword as a consequence of failing in battle or in executing an order from the feudal lords.

As a method of meditation, Zen Buddhism had the function of tranporting the Samurai into a condition of inner quiet so that, at the decisive moment, they were able to use all their energy and overcome fear. Years of practice in the techniques and working on one's own self formed the basic requirements. Perfection could never be reached; instead, the sheer effort brought one a little nearer. Concentration and the ability to rid the mind of other feelings and thoughts were the aim of meditation.

Translated into today's Karate-Do, this would mean that the aim of training would not be towards the highest degree of performance in the sport but would be the "way" – that is, practising. FUNAKOSHI's famous words; "The main aim in the art of Karate is neither winning nor losing; it is the improvement of the character" express this lifelong striving to perfect control of the body and mind. Karate techniques and the rank reached in mastering them is merely a reflection of the inner man at that particular time. "Mushin" – an open mind without having to think – is a mental process, which should help the pupil to progress down this difficult path.

The Japanese Karate masters incorporated several elements of Bushido, such as the rules of behaviour and the high degree of ethical moral demands, stretching well over the bounds of training by continued practice in mastering the martial art throughout one's life. The mental principles were adopted from the influence of Zen-Buddhism anchored in Japanese society and combined with the system of techniques of the original fighting style of the Okinawa-Te, which is free from any philosophy.

FUNAKOSHI expressed of the philosophy of Do in Karate using the 20 'commandment' paragraphs. They serve to help the pupil in his search for perfection and in developing his individual potential. Although practice and training make up the nucleus of the Do, the execution of a practice exercise does not necessarily serve to learn the skill. It serves, above all, to enrich life through awareness and knowledge.

In his book "Shotokan no Hyakkajiten", SCHLATT (1995) lists FUNAKOSHI's 20 principles that define the philosophy of Karate-Do as a model:

- **Never forget: Karate starts with the Rei and ends with the Rei.**
  (Rei means veneration and respect).
- **In Karate there is no pre-emptive strike.**
  (In Karate you don't attack first).

- **Karate aids on the road to fairness.**
- **First of all, know yourself and then others.**
- **Body and spirit come before technique.**
- **Learn to control your body and mind, and keep it clear.**
- **Negligence causes harm.**
- **Karate doesn't take place only in the dojo.**
- **Learning Karate is a life-long task.**
- **Combine your daily routine with Karate – that is the secret.**
- **True Karate is like hot water, which cools rapidly if you don't keep it constantly warm.**
- **Don't think about winning all the time, but think about how not to lose.**
- **Gauge yourself according to your opponent.**
- **The fight depends on exploiting successes and misses.**
- **Imagine your hand and your foot are swords.**
- **When you exit the gateway of youth, you'll find you have many opponents.**
- **Moving to adopt a stance is what beginners do; later, it becomes a natural act.**
- **Practise the Kata correctly; in a real fight it will be another thing.**
- **Hard and soft, tension and relaxation, slow and fast – do everything with the right breathing control.**
- **Always think about what you are doing and constantly try something new.**

Politeness, respect and the defensive characteristics of Karate, which are anchored as the main theme in FUNAKOSHI's principles, are all symbolised in the emblem of Shotokan Karate. The tiger in the circle illustrates the principles of Karate-Do. The tiger represents the ability to fight and to win, but it's freedom and aggressiveness is limited by the confines of the circle. The circle represents patience, consideration, reasonability, understanding, control – the essence of Karate-Do. These characteristics should be your constant companion in your routine, daily training.

1.2   Kata

The Kata contain the whole of the riches of Karate. The large spectrum of techniques, which can be used close up or at medium or long distances, can be found in the Kata. If for no other reason, this is why your training sessions take on serious significance.

The Kata – as already said – concisely express the self-defence techniques of the time when Okinawa-Te was still forbidden in the form of combat against several imaginary opponents. "Form", or the more freely interpreted expression "Sequences", is the correct translation for the term "Kata". After 1900, as interest in Karate was quickly spreading, the contemporary styles we know today came into existence and shaped each of the various systems according to each individual understanding of the art of Kata. This process came to an end at the end of the 1940s. Just how many Kata there are is a hotly debated subject. It is certain that there are at least 80 Kata in existence, and these are practised in numerous different Karate styles.

In Shotokan, there are 26 Kata if one does not count the Taikyoku-Kata preliminary exercise forms. Originally, Gichin FUNAKOSHI selected 15 Kata, which he held as central to the training for Shotokan. They contained the individual typical traditions of the Shorin and Shorei schools. Among these Kata were the basic Kata Heian Shodan, Heian Nidan, Heian Sandan, Heian Yondan and Heian Godan. One assumes that they were developed from the complex Kata Kanku-Dai in order to afford beginners a systematic and simplified introduction to the sequences and techniques.

These basic Kata stem from the Shorin school, whose masters taught the principle of rapid and powerful movements. Originally, they were called "Pinan" Kata until Funakoshi renamed them "Heian", which means "peace" and "calm". For him, the three Tekki-Kata also belonged to the central Kata, such as Bassai-Dai, Kanku-Dai, Empi, Gankaku, Jitte, Hangetsu and Jion. Several additional Kata came later, such as Gojushiho-Kata and Sochin, which FUNAKOSHI had integrated into the Shotokan system by his son Giko and Masatoshi NAKAYAMA. And so we arrive at 26 Kata in Shotokan Karate:

Basic Kata:
Heian 1-5, Tekki 1-3,

Master Kata:
Bassai-Dai, Jion, Empi, Hangetsu, Kanku-Dai

Advanced Master Kata:
Jitte, Meikyu, Ji'in, Bassai-Sho, Kanku-Sho, Gankaku, Chinte, Wankan, Nijushiho, Gojushiho-Sho, Gojushiho-Dai, Sochin, Unsu.

NAKAYAMA laid down in his books the accepted level of techniques, their sequences and application, which are used in Shotokan Kata still today. These had been defined already in 1948 at a meeting of universities in Japan practising Shotokan. The Kata illustrated in these books are primarily drawn from his interpretation.

Each Kata illustrates a strictly defined and complete element and consists of a typical fighting repertoire with a typical rhythm and degree of difficulty. At all times, however, the principle of "Karate ni sente nashi" is maintained; this means: "There is no first attack in Karate". As a result, all Kata begin with a blocking technique. This doesn't exclude that in some Kata, a direct counter can be interpreted as being used as the opponent starts to attack.

As a general rule, and as one moves up the scale, the Kata increase in complexity and in the number of techniques and steps. Thus, the first Kata – Heian Shodan – consists of 21 movements, Heian Nidan has 26 movements and Heian Yondan 27. Common to all the Kata is the fighting shout 'Kiai', which is uttered at specifically set points. This is the way that the whole Kime of the techniques unfolds. The 'Kiai' is uttered at those places in the Kata where a decisive counterattack comes. In the Kata, this means a dramatic highpoint, by which time certain movements must have been successfully executed, e.g., when a "chapter" in the Kata or the whole Kata is completed.

A further common point in the Kata is the presence of a set sequence of steps (Enbusen). This means that direction and sequence have to be always the same. The starting stance must also match the end of the Kata. The Kata always begin with the formal greeting in Musubi-Dachi, the stance where the heels are together. After this, the 'ready' position Hachi-Dachi is adopted. Each change of direction is accompanied and preceded by a change in the direction of the eyes.

Kata training differs between dojos. It is important that, first of all, a good standard of basic techniques is reached before one starts with the actual Kata training. At the beginning, the sequence of the Kata is practised slowly. Correct turns, techniques and stances are now critical, while powerful and dynamic execution comes later. After the sequence has been mastered, these components come into play. Let's add to that: This is when it gets really interesting! Dynamics, rhythm and expression in the Kata performance can only be carried out on the basis of a flawless internalisation of the sequence. The appreciation of the significance of the technique being executed adds yet another dimension.

The fascinating thing about the life-long pursuit of Kata training is the constant increase in new experiences that one can still find in doing the exercises, which you already thought you had learned fully. One can never master a Kata completely. It's more like you will get somewhere near perfecting it. It goes without saying that "perfect" must be seen as a relative statement. Ten different people carrying out the same Kata will execute it in ten different ways. It's not about the sequence of the technique or the rhythm, which are of course set.

Size, weight, stature, body type, age, sex, flexibility and other factors all influence the differences. Every good examiner and competition referee will take these into account in his assessment; he will recognise the individual qualities and grade the Kata performance accordingly, i.e., whether the Karateka has achieved the highest possible advantage from his individual attempt.

Of course, the Kata performance must be correct and bring out the energy, fighting spirit and explosiveness in the right place. The rapid and slow movements as well as tension and relaxation must also be taken into account. Breathing in and breathing out at the correct moments are similarly elementary criteria for the assessment. If a Kata is executed too quickly, its uniqueness is often lost.

Highly ranked Kata experts demonstrate their Kata properly. They can tell a story with their Kata performance that reveals their essence. The practised eye will be able to spot exactly whether the Kata showed "fighting spirit" or whether it merely showed a semblance of a perfectly executed sequence.

One can practice Kata in many different ways. How intensive the applications are executed in training is a question that has many varied answers. The opinion of many Karate trainers is that, in general Karateka who are taking their training seriously will almost always decide for themselves which applications they will use. This is certainly the case for many of the simple blocking and attack techniques. The feeling for other, more complex techniques is not quite so clearly apparent. One has to practice with a partner to understand which application might be the best to use. Many techniques are of a purely symbolic nature, while others must be practised very slowly and with great care in order not to injure the partner. When training for the Bunkai, which is expected in many of the tests, there are as many different opinions as there are possibilities for using each possible application of techniques. And it is also true that this might not be the only correct version.

Thus, just as there are a number of applications for the first movement in the first Kata, it is also important to register that there is no "perfect" solution; rather, each will have its own justification. The same applies to the variety of training methods. It is also quite in order to see the purpose of Kata training more as being general instruction in flexibility, coordination, rhythm, the aesthetics of the movement and, finally, condition. The self-defence aspects can be covered by the classic Karate-Kumite, while the Bunkai can concentrate on other ones.

Training tips for learning the Kata

- **Requirement: All the stances and techniques contained in the Kata have already been mastered.**
- **First of all, practice the sequence slowly, and pay attention to correct movement of the hips.**
- **Practise the change in position (turn) and direction of the eyes.**
- **Timing, power, dynamic and fighting spirit are introduced only after the sequence has been mastered.**
- **After that, the understanding for the application can be increased by training with a partner.**
- **In order to improve the Kata, training in front of a mirror, like those available in many dojos, can be of great assistance.**
- **Individual elements of the Kata should be repeated and practised as long as it takes to master them.**
- **Those Kata that you have already learned should be repeated slowly but with full effort in order to maintain your repertoire.**
- **Don't execute a Kata in a hasty fashion. Katas tell a story. Any good story has an introduction, a high (main) point and a conclusion.**
- **Don't begin a new Kata too soon. The ability to master a Kata takes several months, if not years, and cannot be learned in a short time.**
- **Whenever the opportunity exists, take part in a Kata tournament. They constitute an excellent exercise in testing yourself under stress conditions and in seeing whether you are able to execute them without a mistake.**

Considering these thoughts, I would like to make the point that the higher the rank, the the more comprehensive the repertoire of Kata that must be mastered. In my opinion, training for the sequences and an understanding of timing, coordination and the finer points all come as a priority in Kata training. Moreover, the meaning of each technique must be understood. How far one gets to grips on how the techniques are used in practice depends on the time that one can devote to Karate.

Eventually, the truly well-rounded Karateka has to also be good at the Kumite. Many – even the traditional Karate trainers – see more potential for self-defence in the Kumite skills than is offered by the application of the Kata. Many Kata techniques are – as already mentioned – of a symbolic nature or as a defence or counter against attacks using the old Samurai or Okinawan weapons, which one no longer comes across in everyday life.

Independent from this, whichever main theme one chooses for Kata training and how intensive one wants to get involved in the Bunkai, there is nothing mysterious or secret in the Kata techniques and their practice in the Bunkai form. If there were, this would mean that these were only open to the well-initiated great masters; but they are not and are, instead, used in mainly simple and practical self-defence situations. "Creative Bunkai", which is sometimes carried out today and where an attempt is made to develop a kind of free-fighting from the applications, goes too far away from the direct application of Kata techniques in the opinion of many Kata experts. This is also too far removed from correct Kumite, although this form does find its followers amongst many Karateka.

Independent again from this, whichever main theme you concentrate on in training, an understanding for the Kata takes a lot of time, and not everyone can spend the amount of time on intensively practising Karate-Do that would perhaps be necessary to completely master it. Therefore, you simply have to look at it as a life-long task and not give up if, after several years, you still cannot cover equally all the ground in Karate. Karate-Do is a long-term project and not something that one can master in two or three years.

The study of this fascinating sport of Shotokan Karate is a challenge that can be taken up and mastered by any age group. Kata make it possible to have a life-long practice companion. Unlike other disciplines, in which the zenith of performance is reached at a particular age and when you can no longer improve your times, weight or distances, the conscious practice of the Kata will lead to improvement. An understanding of the wide range of possibilities and dedication to and work on the sequences brings new experiences of many different kinds in every phase of life in Karate.

2   THE BASIC KATA

2.1   Heian Shodan

This is the first Kata taught in most dojos. Heian Shodan allows one to be able to practise the most important aspects of fighting at a medium and long distance. As it does not contain very complicated techniques, it serves, above all, to teach the basic principles of fighting against several opponents attacking from different directions. It also serves to combine the basic techniques learnt already with the correct use of the hip and the way of turning in different directions.

8

9

10

11

12

13

14

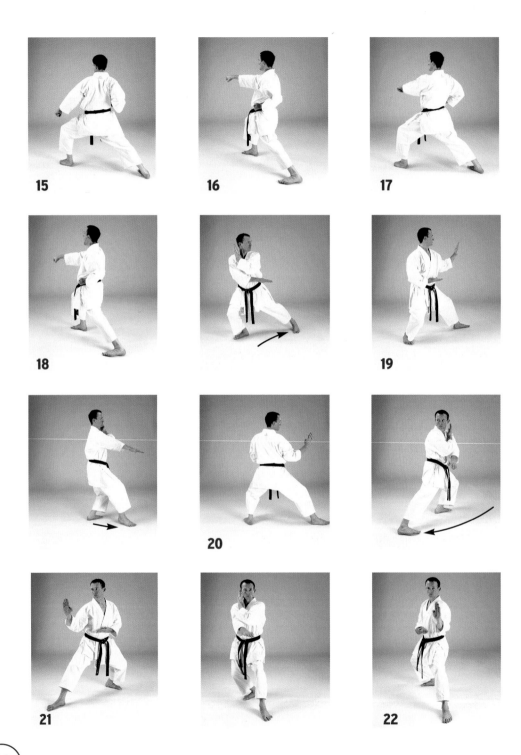

23

Sequence of actions

1   Shizentai. Unless otherwise indicated, all stances are in the Zenkutsu-Dachi position.
2   Go left using a Gedan-Barai.
3   Move forward with a right Oi-Zuki.
4   Turn 180° on the left leg using a right Gedan-Barai.
5   Bring the forward leg backwards in a Renoji-Dachi delivering a right Tettsui-Uchi.
6   Move forward delivering a left Oi-Zuki.
7   Turn 90° to the left and use a left Gedan-Barai.
8   Move forward with a right Age-Uke.
9   Move forward with a left Age-Uke.
10 Move forward with a right Age-Uke and utter a **Kiai**.
11 Turn 270° swivelling on the right leg using a left Gedan-Barai.
12 Move forward with a right Oi-Zuki.
13 Turn 180° swivelling on the right leg using a right Gedan-Barai.
14 Move forward with a left Oi-Zuki.
15 Turn 90° to the left using a left Gedan-Barai.
16 Move forward with a right Oi-Zuki.
17 Move forward with a left Oi-Zuki.
18 Move forward with a right Oi-Zuki and utter a **Kiai**.
19 Turn 270° swivelling on the right leg with a left Shuto-Uke into a Kokutsu-Dachi position.
20 Move forward turning 45° to the right with a Shuto-Uke into a Kokutsu-Dachi position.
21 Move back at an angle of 135° to the main axis with a right Shuto-Uke into a Kokutsu-Dachi position.
22 Move 45° forward with a left Shuto-Uke into a Kokutsu-Dachi position.
23 Shizentai.

HEIAN SHODAN

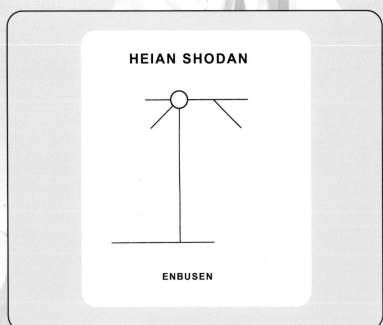

ENBUSEN

Bunkai

1a

1b

Application used for (2)-(3)

2a

2b

Application used for (5)

2c

3a

3b

Application used for (4)-(5)

3c

4a

4b

Application used for (7)-(8)

4c

5a

Application used for (8)-(9)

5b

6a

Application used for (20)-(21)

6b

6c

HEIAN NIDAN

2.2 Heian Nidan

Heian Nidan is a little more complex, although it has a similar foot sequence to Heian Shodan. It uses kicks and defensive techniques at medium and long distances. For the first time, double blocks are used that demand increased flexibility. The techniques in Heian Nidan are notable for providing an interesting potential for self-defence.

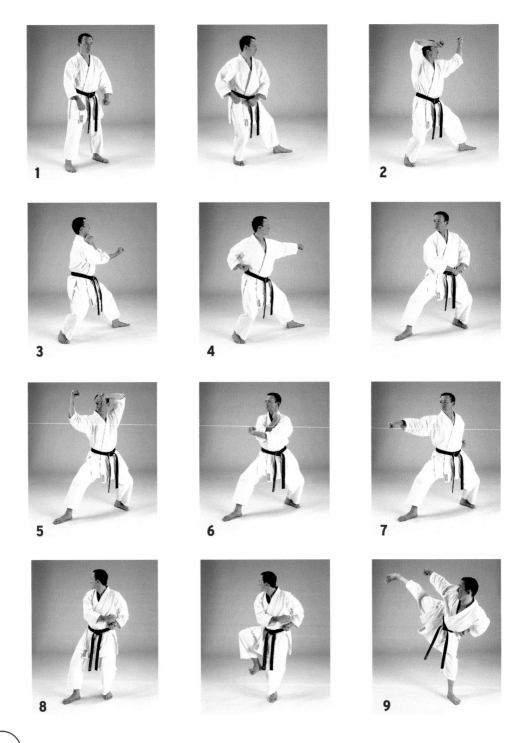

25

26

27

28

29

Sequence of actions

1 Shizentai.

2 Go left leading in a Kokutsu-Dachi position and a double-block in Jodan.

3 Pull the left arm back to the shoulder and execute an Ura-Zuki with the right arm.

4 Counterattack with a left Chudan-Zuki.

5 Bring the fists onto the left hip, one over the other, and move to the right into a Kokutsu-Dachi position with a Jodan double-block.

6 Pull the right arm back to the shoulder and execute an Ura-Zuki with the left arm.

7 Counterattack with a right Chudan-Zuki.

8 Swing back to execute a Yoko-Geri.

9 Execute a right-footed Yoko-Geri with Uraken.

10 Place the foot down in a Kokutsu-Dachi position and do a left Shoto-Uke.

11 Move forward in the Kokutsu-Dachi position with a right Shuto-Uke.

12 Move forward in the Kokutsu-Dachi position with a left Shuto-Uke.

13 Move forward in the Zenkutsu-Dachi position with a right Nukite and utter a **Kiai**.

14 Turn 270° on the right leg in the Kokutsu-Dachi position with a left Shuto-Uke.

15 Move forward into a 45° Kokutsu-Dachi position with a right Shuto-Uke.

16 Go right 135° into the Kokutsu-Dachi position with a right Shuto-Uke.

17 Move forward into a 45° Kokutsu-Dachi position with a left Shuto-Uke.

18 Transfer the left foot forward 45° into a Zenkutsu-Dachi position and execute a right Gyaku-Uchi-Uke.

19 Execute a Mae-Geri with the right leg.

20 Place the foot down and execute a left Gyaku-Zuki.

21 Remaining in the same position, do a left Gyaku-Uchi-Uke.

22 Execute a Mae-Geri with the left leg.

23 Place the foot down and execute a right Gyaku-Zuki.

24 Move forward with a right Morote-Uke into a Zenkutsu-Dachi position.

25 Make a 270° turn swivelling on the right foot into a Zenkutsu-Dachi position with a left Gedan-Barai.

26 Move forward in a 45° angle into a Zenkutsu-Dachi position doing a right Age-Uke.

27 Turn 135°to the right into a Zenkutsu-Dachi position with a right Gedan-Barai.

28 Move forward in a 45° angle and do a left Age-Uke into a Zenkutsu-Dachi position, uttering a **Kiai**.

29 Shizentai.

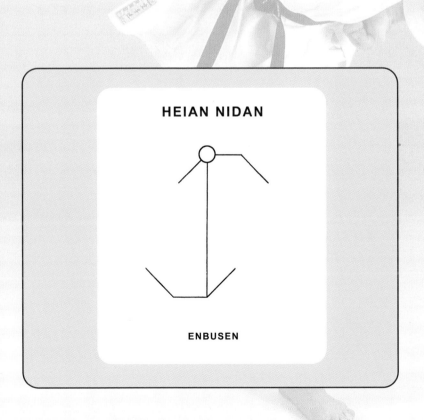

HEIAN NIDAN

ENBUSEN

Bunkai

1a

Application used for (2)-(4)

1b

1c

2a

2b

Application used for (5)-(7)

2c

2d

3a
Application used for (12)-(14)

3b

4a
Application used for (14)-(15)

4b

4c

4d

5a

5b

Application used for (12)-(13)

5c

6a

Application used for (27)-(30)

6b

6c

6d

7a

Application used for (33)-(35)

7b

7c

2.3   Heian Sandan

The difficulty in learning Heian Sandan lies mainly in being able to exactly perform the numerous changes of stance. The prerequisite is to master the basic stances. Besides this, further principles of Karate now come into play: countering against being grabbed at short distance, gliding movements, slow phases with emphasis on breathing and turning over the back into the partner – all these go towards defining the new degree of difficulty of this Kata.

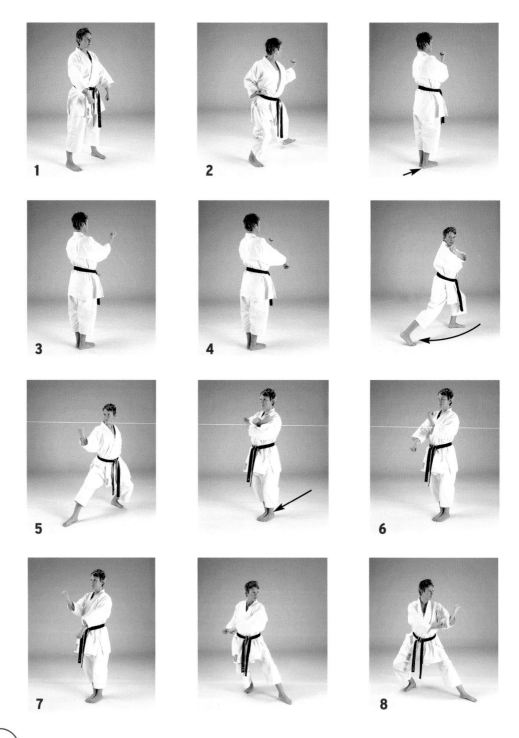

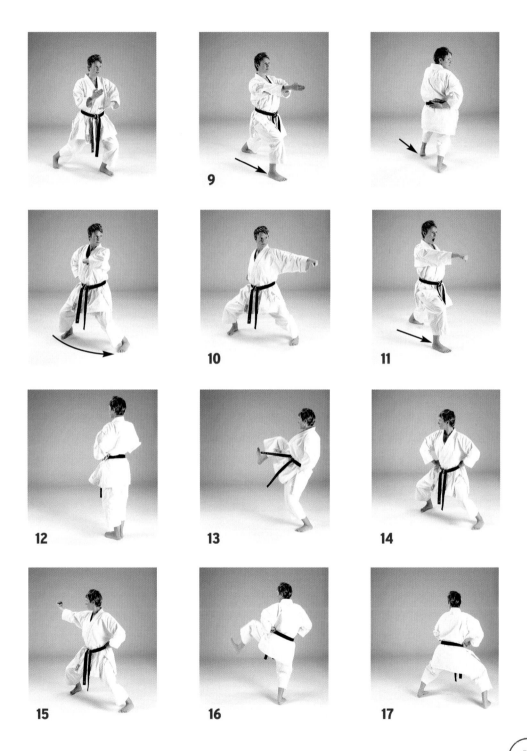

9

10

11

12

13

14

15

16

17

Sequence of actions

1 Shizentai.

2 Go left leading in a Kokutsu-Dachi position with a left Uchi-Uke.

3 Bring the rear leg forwards and stand up executing a right Uchi-Uke and a left Gedan-Barai.

4 Remaining in the same position, execute a left Uchi-Uke and a right Gedan-Barai.

5 Go to the right into a Kokutsu-Dachi position with a right Uchi-Uke.

6 Bring the rear leg forwards and stand upright with a left Uchi-Uke and a right Gedan-Barai.

7 Remaining in the same position, execute a right Uchi-Uke and a left Gedan-Barai.

8 Move forward left 90° with a left Morote-Uke in a Kokutsu-Dachi position.

9 Move forward right in the Zenkutsu-Dachi position with a Nukite.

10 Twist round 360° for a Tettsui-Uchi and do a left Tettsui-Uchi in the Kiba-Dachi position.

11 Move forward in the Zenkutsu-Dachi position with a right Oi-Zuki and utter a **Kiai**.

12 Pull the rear leg in and turn round 180°; stand up and place both fists on the hips.

13 Execute a Fumikomi, leading with the right leg.

14 As the foot sets down, defend right with the elbow...

15 ...and use a right Tate-Uraken.

16 Execute a Fumikomi, leading with the left leg.

17 As the foot sets down, defend left with the elbow...

18 ...and use a left Tate-Uraken.

19 Execute a Fumikomi, leading with the right leg.

20 As the foot sets down, defend right with the elbow...

21 ...and use a right Tate-Uraken.

22 Then, swing back with the right arm to execute a slow Tate-Shuko-Uke.

23 Move forward in the Zenkutsu-Dachi position with a left Oi-Zuki.

24, 25 Bring the rear leg forward alongside the left standing leg; then turn 180° into a Kiba-Dachi position for a Mawashi-Zuki in the Jodan region using a left Empi.

26 Glide back right into a Kiba-Dachi position and, at the same time, execute a left Mawashi-Zuki and a right Empi uttering a **Kiai**.

27 Shizentai.

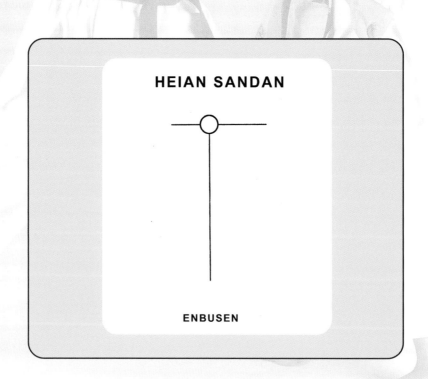

HEIAN SANDAN

ENBUSEN

Bunkai

1a

Application used for (2)-(5)

1b

1c

2a

Application used for (5)-(7)

2b

2c

2d

3a

Application used for (8)-(9)

3b

3c

4a

4b

Application used for (9)-(10)

4c

5a

5b

Application used for (13)-(15)

5c

5d

5e

6a

6b

Application used for (24)-(26)

7a

7b

Application used for (26)

HEIAN YONDAN

2.4   Heian Yondan

The numerous kicks and the advanced requirement of rhythm make Heian Yondan worth watching as an interesting fighting action for medium and long distances as well as for close combat, if well performed. Many of its elements appear again later in the Dan-Kata Kanku-Dai. Heian Yondan also contains many elementary self-defence techniques.

11

12

13

14

15

16

17

18

19

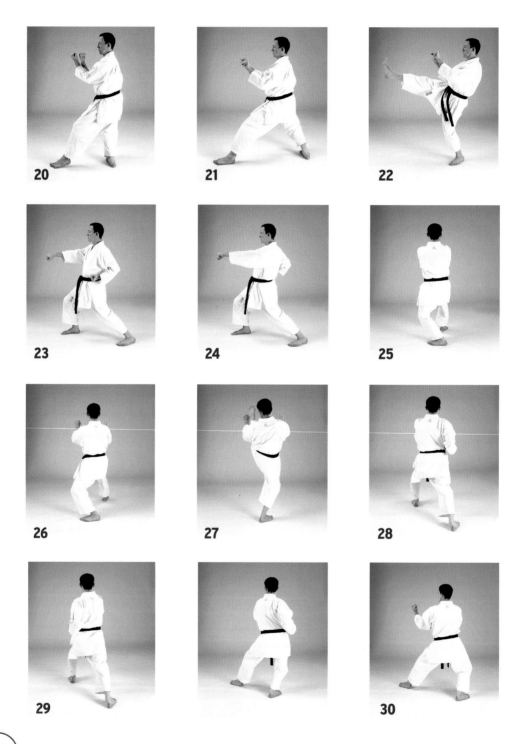

31

32

33

34

35

36

37

Sequence of actions

1 Shizentai.

2 Pull the arms back with open hands to the right as you go forward, left foot leading.

3 Execute an open-handed double-block to the left into a Kokutsu-Dachi position.

4 Go to the right.

5 Push both hands upwards, each with the same, slow movement.

6 Move forward at 90° in the Zenkutsu-Dachi position with a Gedan-Juji-Uke to the left.

7 Move forward right with a Morote-Uke in the Kokutsu-Dachi position.

8 Pull the left leg forwards and bring the fists onto the right hip.

9 Then execute a left-footed Yoko-Geri with Uraken.

10 When snapping back the left leg, the left arm remains with an open hand.

11 Set down the foot in a Zenkutsu-Dachi position and execute a right Mae-Empi.

12 Pull the right leg up to the other and stand upright and with both fists on the left hip, one on the other, . . .

13 . . . to execute a right-footed Yoko-Geri with a right-handed Uraken.

14 When snapping back the right leg, the right arm remains with an open hand, . . .

15 . . . and, when setting down the foot into a Zenkutsu-Dachi position, bring the left Empi (elbow) forwards.

16 From the Zenkutsu-Dachi position, execute a left-arm Gedan-Shuto-Uke and simultaneously bring the right, open hand back to the level of the forehead.

17 Remaining in the same position, move the centre of balance into a left Zenkutsu-Dachi position. As you do, execute a right-handed Jodan Shuto-Uchi and defend left with an open-handed Age-Uke.

18 Go forward and execute a right Mae-Geri.

19 Stretch forwards and place the foot down with a right Uraken in the Kosa-Dachi position, uttering a **Kiai**.

20 Turn 225° on the right foot, and . . .

21 . . . come into a Kaki-Waki-Uke stance in a left Kokutsu-Dachi position.

22 Execute a right-footed Mae-Geri.

23 When setting down the foot, do a right-arm Oi-Zuki.

24 Then do a left-arm Gyaku-Zuki.

25 Right foot forward 90°, . . .

26 . . . into a Kaki-Waki-Uke stance in a Kokutsu-Dachi position.

27 Move forward with left-footed Mae-Geri, . . .

28 . . . and, on setting down the foot, do a left-arm Oi-Zuki.

29 Then do a right-arm Gyaku-Zuki.

30 Move forward 45° in a left Kokutsu-Dachi position with a Morote-Uke.

31 Move forward with a right Morote-Uke into the Kokutsu-Dachi position.

32 Move forward into a left Kokutsu-Dachi position with a Morote-Uke.

33 Change over the left foot into a Zenkutsu-Dachi position and stretch both arms out to the front with open hands.

34 Then execute a Hiza-Geri kick with the right knee and utter a **Kiai**.

35 Turn 180° into a Kokutsu-Dachi position with a left-handed Shuto-Uke defence.

36 Move forwards to the right with a Shuto-Uke into a Kokutsu-Dachi position.

37 Shizentai.

HEIAN YONDAN

ENBUSEN

Bunkai

1a
Application used for (3)

1b

2a
Application used for (6)-(7)

2b

3a
Application used for (8)-(11)

3b

3c

3d

4a

4b

Application used for (16)-(19)

4c

4d

4e

5a

5b

Application used for (32)-(34)

5c

5d

6a

Application used for (34)-(35)

6b

6c

2.5　　　HEIAN GODAN

2.5　Heian Godan

The last of the Heian Kata is, of course, also the hardest. This is not only because of the jumping movement, which is in the sequence, but also on account of the numerous blocks with both arms and the rapid change of positions that is required.

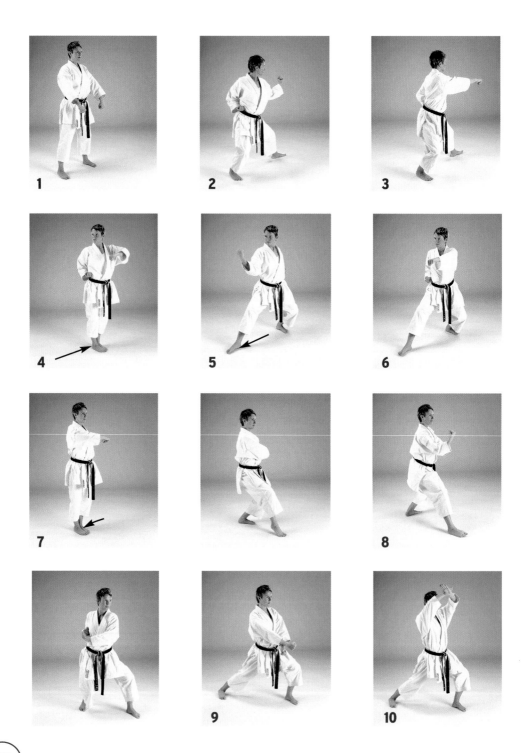

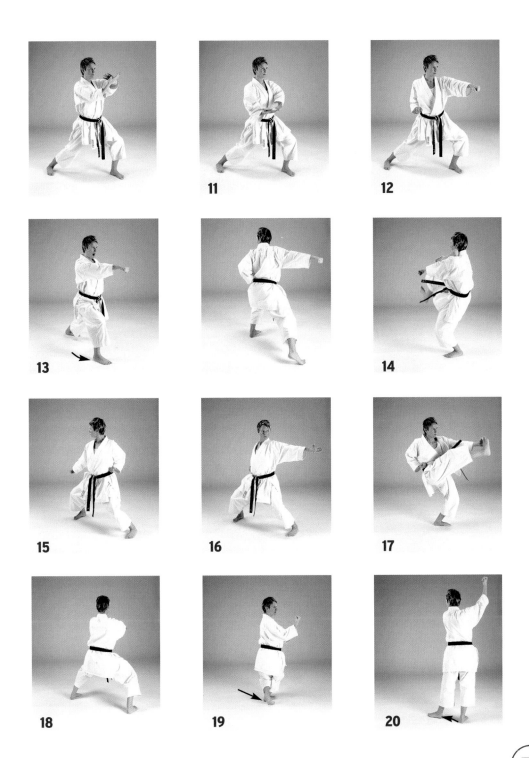

21

22

23

24

25

26

27

28

29

Sequence of actions

1   Shizentai.

2   Go to the left with a left Uchi-Uke into the Kokutsu-Dachi position.

3   Staying in the same position, do a right Gyaku-Zuki.

4   Slowly stand upright with a left-handed Kagi-Zuki, at the same looking to the right.

5   Go to the right with a right Uchi-Uke into the Kokutsu-Dachi position.

6   Staying in the same position, do a left Gyaku-Zuki.

7   Slowly stand upright with a right-handed Kagi-Zuki and direct your eyes to the front.

8   Move forward at 90° with a right Morote-Uke into the Kokutsu-Dachi position.

9   Move forward to the left with a Gedan-Juji-Uke block into the Zenkutsu-Dachi position.

10 Remaining in the same position, strike upwards with open hands for a Jodan-Juji-Uke block.

11 Close the hands and bring them back down onto the right-hand side of the body.

12 Defend using a left-handed Tate-Shuto-Uke.

13 Move forwards with a right-handed Oi-Zuki in the Zenkutsu-Dachi position and utter a **Kiai**.

14 Turn 180° while executing a right Fumikomi in the other direction . . .

15 . . . and, as the foot is placed down, do a Gedan-Barai with the right arm.

16 Stretch the left arm out for a Heishu-Uke in the other direction.

17 Do a Mikazuki-Geri onto the left hand, which is left where it is.

18 On setting the foot down into a Kiba-Dachi position, use a right Empi.

19 Pull the left leg up to the other one and execute a right Morote-Uke into the Kosa-Dachi position.

20 Stand up with a Morote-Ura-Zuki using the right arm while looking to the left.

21 Jump up. At the same time, lift the right knee up rapidly, jump and rip the arms back to the hips.

22 Land with a Gedan-Juji-Uke block, uttering a **Kiai**.

23 Go to the right with a Morote-Uke into the Zenkutsu-Dachi position.

24 Turn 180° with a right-handed Gedan-Nukite and a left-handed Te-Nagashi-Uke into the Zenkutsu-Dachi position.

25 Change into the Kokutsu-Dachi position with a Manji-Uke.

26 Then bring the forward leg back into the Heisoku-Dachi position.

27 Move forward into the Zenkutsu-Dachi position and do a Nukite, this time with the left hand. Block right with a Te-Nagashi-Uke.

28 Change into the Kokutsu-Dachi position with a Manji-Uke.

29 Shizentai.

HEIAN GODAN

ENBUSEN

Bunkai

1a

Application used for (2)-(4)

1b

1c

2a

Application used for (5)-(7)

2b

77

2c

3a

Application used for (9)-(13)

3b

3c

3d

3e

4a

Application used for (16)-(18)

4b

4c

5a

5b

Application used for (19)-(20)

6a

6b

Application used for (23)-(25)

6c

3 THE TEKKI-KATA

3.1 Tekki-Shodan

This new section starts off with Tekki Shodan. Usually one learns the first Tekki-Kata for the brown belt and then the second and third one later after the first Dan. FUNAKOSHI, however, included all three Tekki-Kata in the 15 basic Kata. Because of the interesting potential of their self-defensive elements in close combat, it is worthwhile already coming to grips with Tekki 2 and Tekki 3 at an early stage. In any case, they have a similar basic structure to the Tekki 1. Uniquely, the Tekki-Kata are structured in a completely different way than the Heian Kata and all other Shotokan Kata due to the sequence of steps they employ. While maintaining a movement along a straight line, the techniques are carried out either to the right, to the left or forwards. The basic principle of the three Kata is illustrated by considering defensive manoeuvres in a narrow passage, where there is no room to make turns or carry out a radical change of direction. Kiba-Dachi is the basic stance, and you have to pay particular attention when carrying out the techniques that the hips stay at the same height. The stable and firm Kiba-Dachi stance must not be affected by the arm techniques, change of direction of the eyes and body movement, which are generally all executed sideways. They are sometimes known as the "Iron Riders" as they were originally done on horseback; hence the Kiba-Dachi stance. The ancient name was "Naihanchi", which means "in the middle of the battlefield".

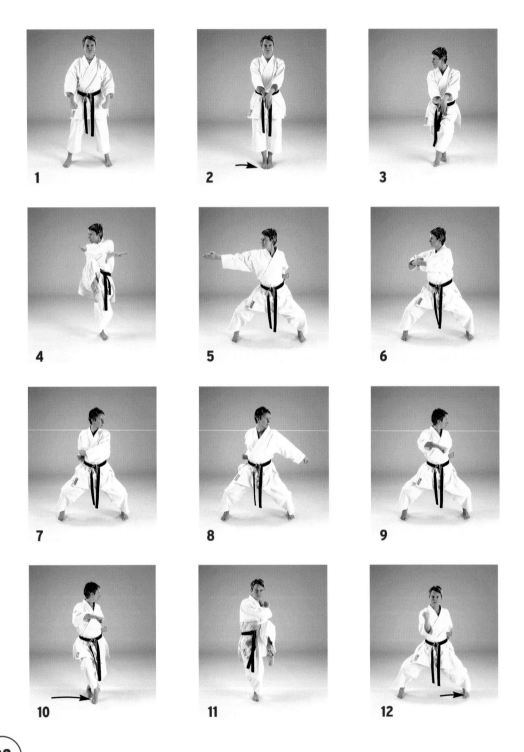

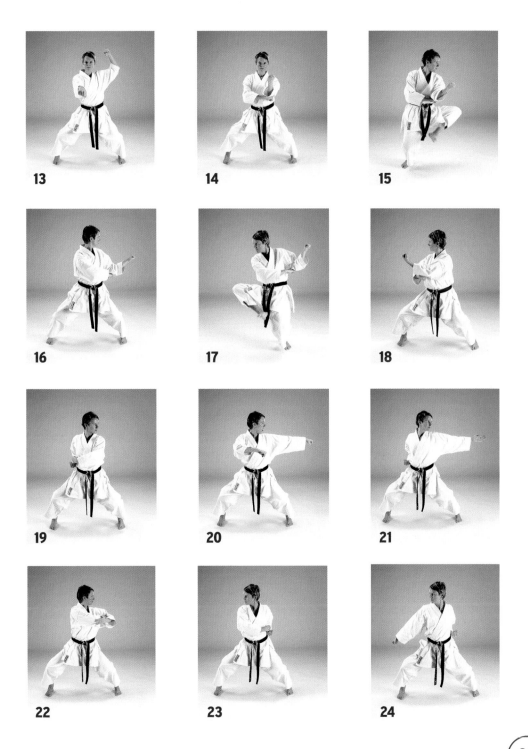

25

26

27

28

29

30

31

32

33

34

35

36

37 →   → 38

Sequence of actions

1 Shizentai. Unless otherwise indicated, all stances are in the Kiba-Dachi position.

2 Place the feet together pulling in the right foot. Place the right hand under the left.

3 Cross the left leg over the other. Look right.

4 Right foot forward and execute the start of a Fumikomi knee-lift.

5 Place the foot down and carry out a right-handed Haishu-Uke.

6 Remaining in the same position grasp the Empi with the right hand.

7 Pull back both fists, one over the other, onto the right hip and look left.

8 Then block with a Gedan-Barai with the left arm.

9 Swing into a Kagi-Zuki with the right arm.

10 Transfer into a Kosa-Dachi position.

11 Stretch forward and round with the right arm and snap the left knee forward.

12 Place the leg down with a right-handed Uchi-Uke.

13 Carry out a right-handed Gedan-Uke and simultaneously defend with a Jodan Nagashi-Uke.

14 Execute an Ura-Zuki with the left arm.

15 Look left and defend with a Nami-Ashi.

16 Place the leg down again and do a Morote-Uke.

17 Defend with a right-footed Nami-Ashi . . .

18 . . . and go to the right with a Morote-Uke.

19 Pull back both fists onto the right hip.

20 Carry out a left-handed Chudan-Zuki and a Kagi-Zuki with the right arm ending with a **Kiai**.

21 Slowly stretch the left arm out and execute a left-handed Haishu-Uke.

22 Grasp the Empi with the right hand.

23 Look right. Pull the fists back rapidly onto the left hip.

24 Execute a right-handed Gedan-Uke.

25 Kagi-Zuki with the left arm.

26 Slowly switch into a Kosa-Dachi position.

27 Raise the right knee rapidly and pull back with the left arm.

28 Place the foot down again and defend with a left-arm Uchi-Uke.

29 Execute a left-handed Gedan-Barai while at the same time pulling back right for a Jodan-Nagashi-Uke.

30 Deliver a right-handed Ura-Zuki.

31 Look right and then defend with a Nami-Ashi.

32 Place the foot down again with a Morote-Uke.

33 Execute a Nami-Ashi to the left...

34 ...and to the right with a Morote-Uke.

35 Pull back both fists onto the left hip...

36 ...and then execute a right-handed Chudan-Zuki and a Kagi-Zuki with the left arm ending with a **Kiai**.

37 Bring the arms together, placing the left hand over the right hand.

38 Shizentai.

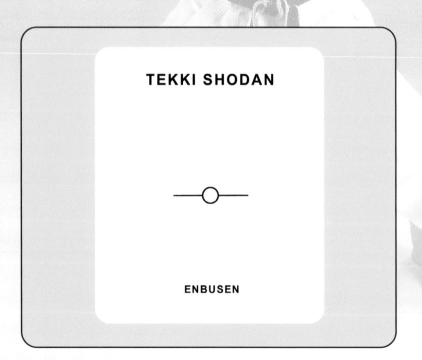

TEKKI SHODAN

ENBUSEN

Bunkai

1a

1b

Application used for (1)-(9)

1c

1d

1e

1f

1g

2a

2b

Application used for (12)-(14)

2c

3a

3b

Application used for (17)-(18)

4a

4b

Application used for (21)-(22)

3.2   TEKKI-NIDAN

3.2   Tekki-Nidan

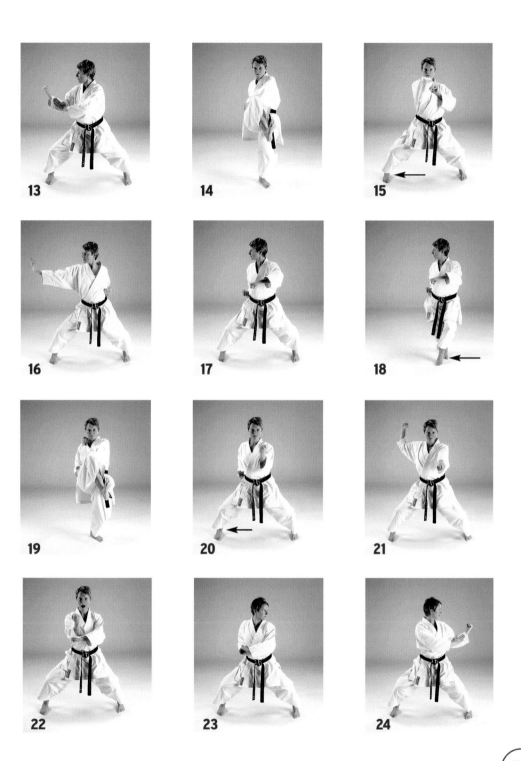

25

26

27

28

29

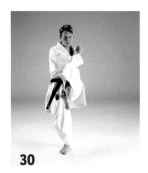

30

31

32

33

34

Sequence of actions

1   Shizentai. Unless otherwise indicated, all stances are in the Kiba-Dachi position.

2   Make a crossover step to the right, and at the same time lift up the arms slowly into a horizontal position and look to the right.

3   Bring up the lower arms together, lifting the right knee up rapidly.

4   Place the foot down and carry out a right-handed Chudan-Uke-Kamae.

5   Make a crossover step to the right.

6   Carry out a low-defensive Gedan-Uke block; the left hand is open and rests in the hollow of the right elbow.

7   Pull the left leg slowly into the right one and look left, lifting the arms up horizontally at the same time.

8   Lift the left knee up rapidly, crossing over the left foot and bring the lower arms together.

9   Place the leg back down with a left-handed Chudan-Uke-Kamae.

10   Take a crossover step to the left side, bringing the right hand into the hollow of the left elbow.

11   Execute a left-handed Gedan-Uke defensive block.

12   Look to the right, placing the right fist into the left hand on the left hip.

13   Defend with a right arm Uchi-Uke, supported by the left hand.

14   Pull the right fist back quickly, covering it with the open left hand, and at the same time lift up the right knee rapidly.

15   Place the foot down and do a right Mae-Empi; the fist stays cradled in the right hand.

16   With the right hand, slowly execute a Tate-Shuto-Uke to the right.

17   Do a left Kagi-Zuki.

18   Crossover step to the right.

19   Lift the right knee up rapidly, bringing the left arm back around for an Uchi-Uke. Look straight forwards.

20   Place the foot down and do an Uchi-Uke to the left . . .

21   . . . while you simultaneously defend with a right-handed Jodan-Nagashi-Uke and a left Gedan-Uke.

22   Execute an Ura-Zuki with the right arm and utter a **Kiai**.

23   Look left and place the left fist in the right hand.

24   Left Uchi-Uke, supported by the right hand.

25   Lift the left knee up rapidly, snap the left fist back onto the hip and cover it with the right hand. Look straight forward.

26   Place the foot down and do a left Mae-Empi.

27   Look left and slowly execute a Tate-Shuto-Uke.

28   Kagi-Zuki with the right arm.

29 Crossover step to the left.

30 Look straight ahead and pull the right arm back across the body, while lifting up the left knee rapidly.

31 Place the foot down and do a right arm Uchi-Uke . . .

32 . . . while defending with a left-handed Jodan-Nagashi-Uke and a right Gedan Uke.

33 Execute an Ura-Zuki with the left arm and utter a **Kiai**.

34 Bring the right leg up to the other in a Shizentai position.

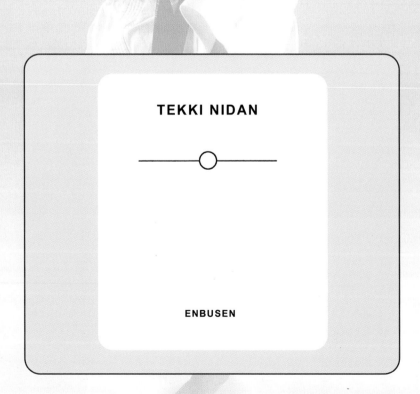

TEKKI NIDAN

ENBUSEN

Bunkai

Application used for (1)-(2)

1c

2a

2b

Application used for (5)-(6)

3a

3b

Application used for (13)-(15)

3c

4a

4b

Application used for (30)-(33)

4c

4d

3.3   TEKKI-SANDAN

3.3   Tekki-Sandan

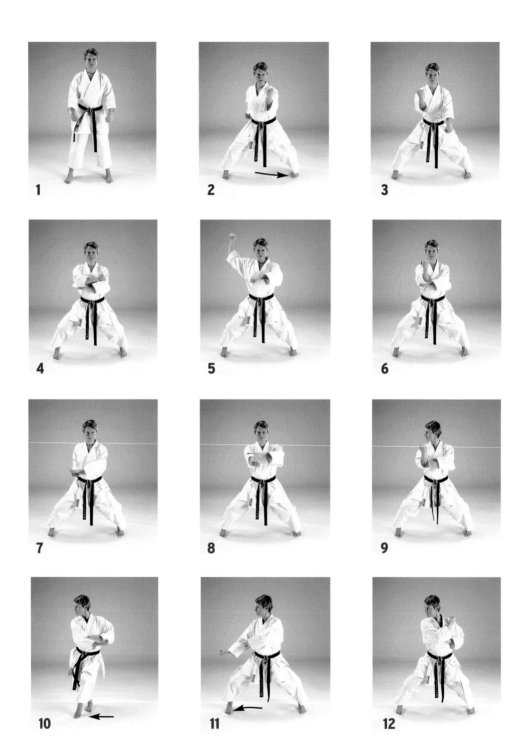

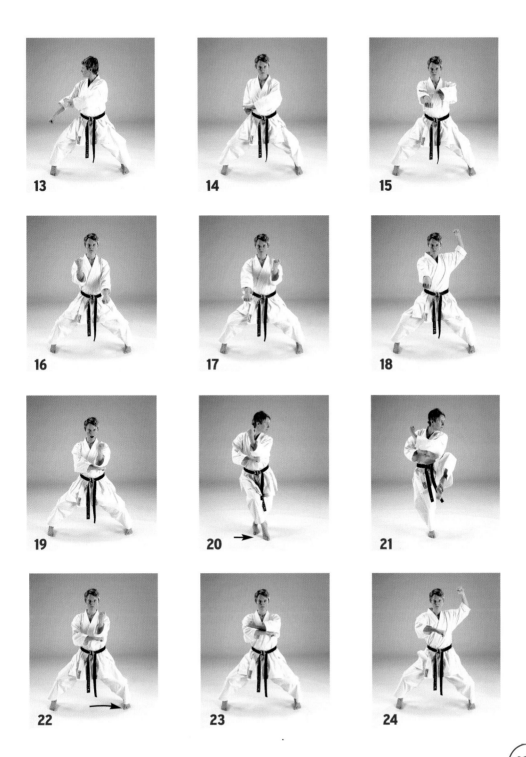

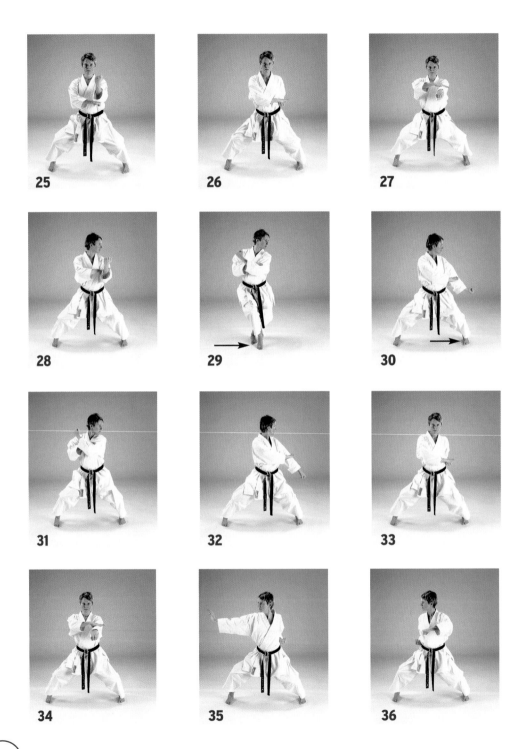

37

38

39

40

41

42

43

Sequence of actions

1　Shizentai. Unless otherwise indicated, all stances are in the Kiba-Dachi position.
2　Place the right foot out to the right in a Kiba-Dachi position defending with a left-arm Uchi-Uke.
3　Then defend with a right-arm Uchi-Uke while at the same time blocking with a left-arm Gedan-Barai.
4　Lay your arms over each other; the right arm is on the top, and the back of your fists are pointing forward.
5　Defend with a right-handed Jodan-Nagashi-Uke.
6　Execute an Ura-Zuki with the right arm; the left arm supports the right elbow.
7　Bring the right fist back onto the hip with a rapid movement; the left hand is placed on the right fist with the back of the hand pointing upwards.
8　Attack with a right Chudan-Zuki underneath the open left hand.
9　Angle the right arm and turn the lower arm over; look right.
10　Crossover step to the right. Bring your left arm forward and around for a right-arm Gedan-Uke block.
11　Do a right Gedan-Uke; the left hand is placed in the hollow of the right elbow; the right arm is not fully stretched out.
12　The right arm is carried across and past the head in a large circular movement into a striking stance.
13　Strike downwards with the back of the hand pointing upwards. The right arm is stretched out, and the left hand remains in its original position.
14　Pull the right fist back onto the hip with a rapid movement and cover it with the open left hand.
15　A right Chudan-Zuki underneath the open left hand.
16　A right Uchi-Uke and, at the same time, a left Gedan-Barai.
17　Change over to a left Uchi-Uke and a right Gedan-Barai.
18　Defend with a left-handed Jodan-Nagashi-Uke.
19　Execute an Ura-Zuki with the left arm and utter a **Kiai**, placing the right arm under the left elbow as support.
20　Look left as you do a slow crossover step to the left. The arms remain unchanged.
21　Lift up the left knee rapidly.
22　Place the foot down while executing a Fumikomi. Look straight ahead keeping the arms in the same position.
23　Lay your arms over each other; the left arm is on the top, and the back of the fist is pointing forwards.
24　Defend with a left-handed Jodan-Nagashi-Uke.
25　Execute an Ura-Zuki with the left arm, placing the right arm under the left elbow as support.
26　Pull the left fist back onto the hip with a rapid movement and cover it with the open right hand.
27　A left Chudan-Zuki underneath the open right hand.
28　Angle the left arm and turn the lower arm over; look left.

29	Crossover step to the left. Bring the left arm back and around for a left-arm Gedan-Uke block.
30	Do a left Gedan-Uke; the right hand is placed in the hollow of the left elbow; the left arm is not fully stretched out.
31	The left arm is carried across and past the head in a large circular movement into a striking stance.
32	Strike downwards with the back of the hand pointing upwards. The left arm is stretched out and the right hand remains in its original position.
33	Pull the left fist back onto the hip with a rapid movement and cover it with the open right hand.
34	A left Chudan-Zuki underneath the open right hand.
35	Look right and, with the right hand, slowly execute a Tate-Shuto-Uke to the right.
36	Do a left Kagi-Zuki.
37	Do a slow crossover step to the right. The arms remain unchanged.
38	Lift the right knee up rapidly, bringing the left arm back around onto the right shoulder.
39	Look straight ahead. Place the foot down doing a Fumikomi and execute a left Uchi-Uke.
40	Do a right Uchi-Uke and, at the same time, a left Gedan-Barai block.
41	Defend with a right-handed Jodan-Nagashi-Uke.
42	Execute an Ura-Zuki with the right arm uttering a **Kiai** and placing the left arm under the right elbow as support.
43	Shizentai.

TEKKI SANDAN

ENBUSEN

Bunkai

1a

Application used for (2)-(6)

1b

1c

1d

1e

2a

Application used for (11)-(13)

2b

2c

The Basic Master Kata

When you have learned the Kata as far as Tekki, then studying the Master Kata begins. These are the Kata that one must master for the 1st Dan. They are longer than the previous ones and consist of numerous techniques and principles that demand longer training times and the perfection of the earlier Kata.

4 BASIC MASTER KATA

4.1 Bassai-Dai

Bassai-Dai is the favourite Kata for the grading test for the 1st Dan. It is characterised by a very complex sequence of movements compared to the Heian-Kata and Tekki. With its rapid and dynamic movements from the hip area, and by employing various blocks, it requires intensive practice. The meaning of the words in its name "Bassai-Dai" is "to storm the fortress", and this describes its powerful character. Bassai-Dai belongs to the basic repertoire in Shotokan Karate, and this has to be learned and mastered for the brown belt and higher. This Kata appears again and again and has to be practised in advanced exercises by the Karateka because it contains the key elements of the style, such as the dynamic use of the hips when executing the Chudan blocks.

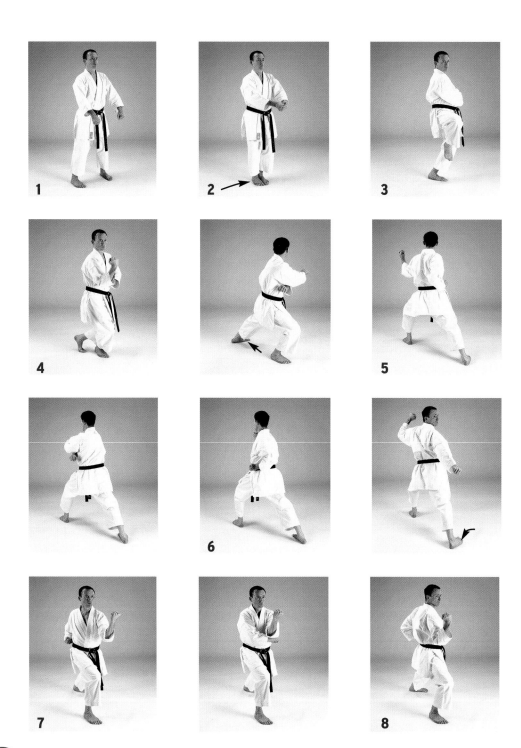

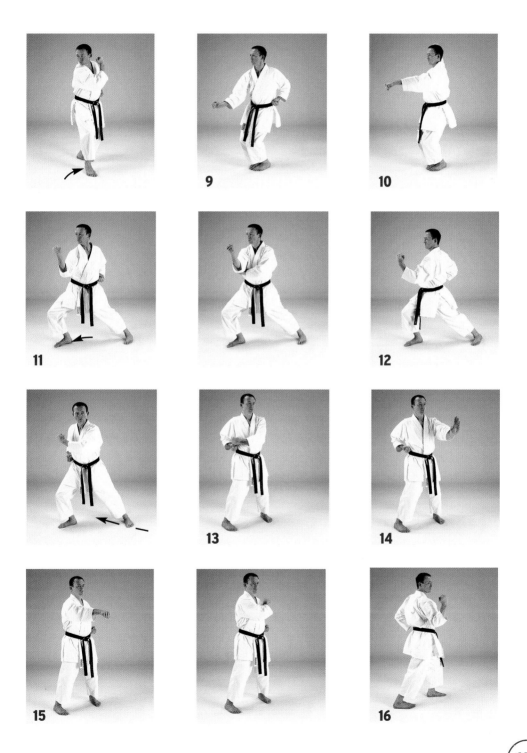

26

27

28

29

30

31

32

33

34

35

36

37

38

39

40

41

42

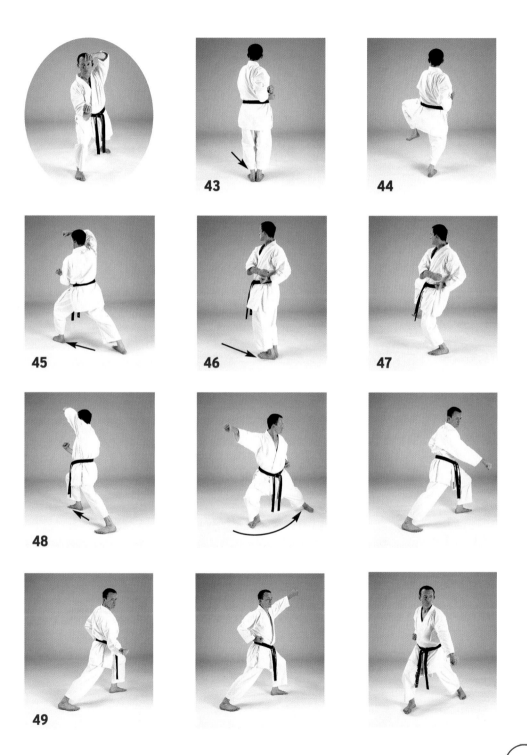

43

44

45

46

47

48

49

50

51

52

53

54

55

56

57

Sequence of actions

1. Shizentai.
2. Bring the feet together with the right coming alongside the left, while at the same time wrapping the left hand round the right clenched fist.
3. Make a spring-step forward leading with a rapid movement of the right knee.
4. Place the foot down into a Kosa-Dachi position and deliver a Morote-Uke.
5. Turn round 180° into a Zenkutsu-Dachi position with a left-handed Uchi-Uke.
6. Remaining in the same position, execute a right-handed Gyaku-Uchi-Uke.
7. Turn round 180° into a Zenkutsu-Dachi position with a left-handed Gyaku-Soto-Uke.
8. Remaining in the same position, execute a right-handed Uchi-Uke.
9. Pull the left leg forward and do a scoop block in the Gedan region.
10. Stretch out the left arm and bring the right arm back level with the right ear.
11. Move forward in the Zenkutsu-Dachi position with the right leg and block with a right-handed Soto-Uke.
12. Remaining in the same position, execute a left-handed Gyaku-Uchi-Uke.
13. Look left. Pull the left foot forwards and pull back both fists joined together onto the right hip. Adopt the Hachi-Dachi position.
14. Remaining in the same position; stretch out the left arm slowly into the Tate-Shuto-Uke posture.
15. Execute a right-handed Choku-Zuki.
16. Turn the right hip forwards executing a right-handed Uchi-Uke block.
17. Bring the hips forward parallel, executing a left-handed Choku-Zuki.
18. Twist the hips, executing a left-handed Uchi-Uke block.
19. Move forward into a right-footed Kokutsu-Dachi position with a Shuto-Uke.
20. Move forward into a left-footed Kokutsu-Dachi position with a Shuto-Uke.
21. Move forward into a right-footed Kokutsu-Dachi position with a Shuto-Uke.
22. Move back into a left-footed Kokutsu-Dachi position with a Shuto-Uke.
23. Change over into a Zenkutsu-Dachi position with a Tsukami-Uke.
24. Pull the right knee up between the angled arms.
25. Execute a Yoko-Geri-Kekomi in the Gedan region uttering a **Kiai**. As you make the step, clench the fists and pull them sharply into the body.
26. Immediately turn around backwards into the Kokutsu-Dachi position with a Shuto-Uke.
27. Move forwards into a right-footed Kokutsu-Dachi position with a Shuto-Uke.
28. Bring the forward leg slowly backwards with a Morote-Uke in the Jodan region.
29. Execute a right Hiza-Geri, ripping the arms apart.
30. Place the foot down firmly in a Sochin-Dachi manner, executing a Hasami-Uchi.
31. Slip forward into the Zenkutsu-Dachi position with an Oi-Zuki strike.

32 Turn around 180° into a left-footed Zenkutsu-Dachi position, executing a right-handed Gedan-Nukite.

33 Bring the forward left leg slowly backwards to the standing leg with a right-handed Uchi-Uke in the Jodan region and a left-handed Gedan-Barai block.

34 Move forwards with a right Fumikomi knee-lift. As the right knee is lifted, pull the right fist in a Gedan-Barai onto the left shoulder.

35 The foot comes down in a Kiba-Dachi position.

36 In the same position, stretch the arm forwards and go in the other direction executing a Haisho-Uke.

37 Execute a right-footed Mikazuki-Geri; the foot hits the stretched-out left hand.

38 Placing the foot down into the Kiba-Dachi position, execute a right-sided Mae-Empi.

39 Remaining in the same position, defend with a right-handed Gedan-Uke.

40 Remaining in the same position, defend with a left-handed Gedan-Uke.

41 Remaining in the same position, defend with a right-handed Gedan-Uke.

42 Switch around to the right into a Zenkutsu-Dachi position, executing a Yama-Zuki after having brought the fists from the left hip, where they had been held for a short time.

43 Bring back the forward leg slowly and pull back the fists onto the right hip. The feet are angled 45° to the right.

44 Go forward again, executing a left-footed Hiza-Geri.

45 Yama-Zuki (on landing with the foot) in the Zenkutsu-Dachi position; now with the left leg forward.

46 Pull the forward leg back slowly and pull back both fists onto the hip. The feet are angled 45° to the left.

47 Go forward again, executing a right-footed Hiza-Geri.

48 Yama-Zuki (on landing with the foot) into the Zenkutsu-Dachi position. Right leg forward.

49 Turn around 270° on the right leg, pulling back hard with the left arm in a large movement. Then defend downwards with a right-handed Sukui-Uke.

50 Execute the same movement, this time left-handed Sukui-Uke.

51 Then pull the left leg to the right one and move forward right 45° into a Kokutsu-Dachi position with a Shuto-Uke.

52 With the right foot, trace a small half-circle and, after placing it down to the rear, move into a 90° angle without changing the technique; only the head and the eyes change direction.

53 Stand in a Kokutsu-Dachi position with a right-handed Shuto-Uke. Look in the opposite direction to the technique, i.e., rearwards.

54 Pull the feet together, rearwards to the other.

55 Go forward with a left-handed Shuto-Uke into a Kokutso-Dachi position and utter a **Kiai**.

56 Bring the forward leg back and place the right-hand fist in the left hand again.

57 Shizentai.

BASSAI-DAI

ENBUSEN

Bunkai

1a

Application used for (2)-(4)

1b

1c

2a

Application used for (5)-(7)

2b

2c

3a 3b

Application used for (9)-(14)

4a 4b

Application used for (13)-(18)

4c

4d

4e

5a

Application used for (23)-(25)

5b

5c

5d

5e

6a

Application used for (28)-(31)

6b

6c

6d

6e

7a

7b

Application used for (42)-(45)

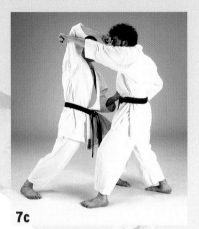

7c

8a

Application used for (49)-(50)

8b

4.2   Jion

Jion is a very powerful Kata derived from the Shorei tradition. It is usually taught as the second Kata after Bassai-Dai. Technically, it is not particularly demanding. You must be able to master the change in positions in the Kiba-Dachi, Zenkutsu-Dachi and Kokutsu-Dachi in order to be able to carry out Jion reasonably well. Talking about this Kata, Hirokazu KANAZAWA remarks: "Earlier, one believed that this Kata came from China because the Buddhist expression 'Jion' was to be found in old Chinese literature. One also found that, in the Jion Temple, martial arts were practised intensively. I believe that this Kata stems from the Jion Temple, was then introduced into the Tomari region of Okinawa and spread from there. Jion actually means 'love and gratitude'." KANAZAWA compares the movement in Jion with the "full ripeness of the Buddha".

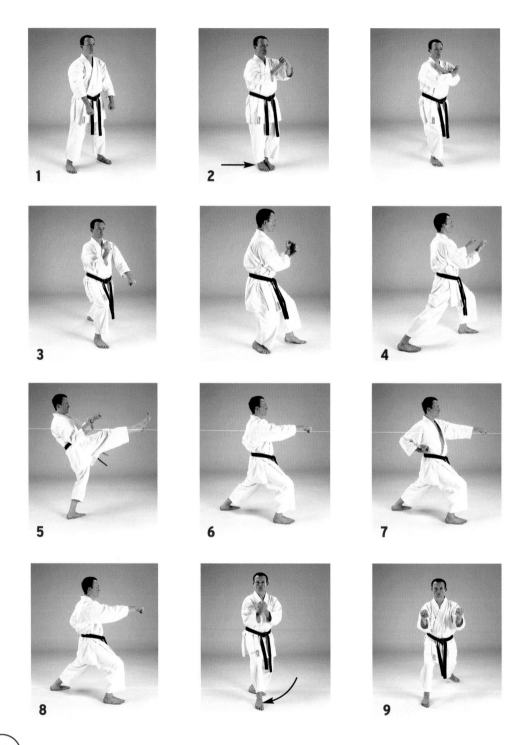

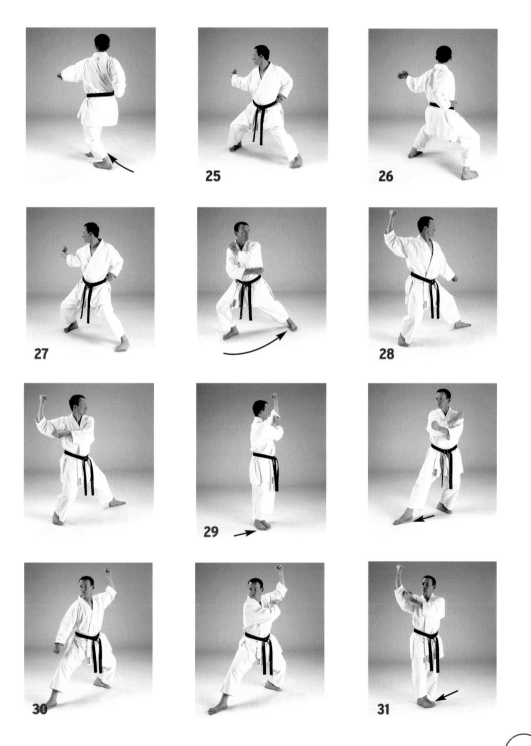

25

26

27

28

29

30

31

42

43

44

45

46

47

48

49

50

51

Sequence of actions

1 Shizentai.

2 Slowly bring the right foot together alongside the left in a Heisoku-Dachi position while at the same time laying the left hand over the right fist.

3 Bring back the left leg into a Zenkutsu-Dachi position and execute a right-handed Uchi-Uke and a left Gedan-Barai.

4 Go left slowly in a 45° angle into a Zenkutsu-Dachi position with a Kaki-Wake-Uke hook.

5 Kick forward right in a Mae-Geri; the arms remain unchanged.

6 Place the foot down moving forward with a right-handed Oi-Zuki into a Zenkutsu-Dachi position.

7 Remaining in the same position, execute a left-handed Gyaku-Zuki.

8 Remaining in the same position, execute a right-handed Zuki.

9 Slowly go in a 90° angle to the right into a Zenkutsu-Dachi position with a Kaki-Wake-Uke hook.

10 Kick forward left in a Mae-Geri; the arms remain unchanged.

11 Place the foot down moving forward with a left-handed Oi-Zuki into a Zenkutsu-Dachi position.

12 Remaining in the same position, execute a right-handed Gyaku-Zuki.

13 Remaining in the same position, execute a left-handed Zuki.

14 Change over into a 45° angle forward and go to the left into a Zenkutsu-Dachi position; before this, pull the open right hand back for a left arm Age-Uke block into the Zenkutsu-Dachi position.

15 Remaining in the same position, execute a right-handed Gyaku-Zuki.

16 Move forward into a Zenkutsu-Dachi position doing a right arm Age-Uke block.

17 Remaining in the same position, execute a left-handed Gyaku-Zuki.

18 Move forward into a Zenkutsu-Dachi position doing a left-arm Age-Uke block.

19 Move forward into a Zenkutsu-Dachi position with a right-arm Oi-Zuki attack and utter a **Kiai**.

20 Turn around on the right foot 270° into a Kokutsu-Dachi position with a Manji-Uke.

21 Slide the left leg forwards into a Kiba-Dachi position, doing a right arm Kagi-Zuki.

22 Move your balance to the left and execute a Manji-Uke into a Kokutsu-Dachi position. Look right.

23 Slide to the right into a Kiba-Dachi position, doing a left arm Kagi-Zuki.

24 Go forward in a 90° angle into a Zenkutsu-Dachi position with a left-handed Gedan-Barai block.

25 Move forward into Kiba-Dachi position with the right palm in a Teisho.

26 Move forward into Kiba-Dachi position with the left palm in a Teisho.

27 Move forward with the right palm in a Teisho.

28 Turn around on the right foot 270° into a Kokutsu-Dachi position with a left Manji-Uke.

29 Pull the right leg up to the other one while doing a left Jodan Morote-Uke.

30 Turn around 180° to the right into a Kokutsu-Dachi position with a right Manji-Uke.

31 Pull the left leg up to the other one while doing a right Jodan-Morote-Uke.

32 Look straight forward while, at the same time, slowly crossing the arms over, pulling them down and stretching them out sideways in a Kamae guard position.

33 Do a right-knee Hiza-Geri, pulling both fists back to the hips.

34 Place the foot down into a Kosa-Dachi position with a crossed-arm Gedan-Juji-Uke block. The right-hand fist is placed over the left one.

35 Bring the left leg backwards into a Zenkutsu-Dachi position while doing a right Gedan-Kaki-Wake-Uke.

36 Go forward into a Zenkutsu-Dachi position with a double Uchi-Uke.

37 Go forward into a Zenkutsu-Dachi position with a Jodan-Juji-Uke.

38 Execute a reverse right-arm Uraken-Uchi and then a sweeping Jodan-Nagashi-Uke punch block.

39 Stretch the left arm forwards and execute a right-fisted Jodan-Nagashi-Uke sweeping punch block.

40 Execute a right-fisted Jodan-Ura-Zuki punch.

41 Turn around on the right foot 270° into a Zenkutsu-Dachi position with a left Uchi-Uke.

42 Go forward with a right-strike Oi-Zuki into a Zenkutsu-Dachi position.

43 Turn around to the rear 180° into a Zenkutsu-Dachi position with a right Uchi-Uke.

44 Go forward with a left-strike Oi-Zuki into a Zenkutsu-Dachi position.

45 Turn around to the left 90° into a Zenkutsu-Dachi position with a left Gedan-Barai.

46 Lift the right knee up rapidly and stretch both arms out.

47 Place the foot down with a right-footed Fumikomi and execute an Otoshi-Uke thrust into a Kiba-Dachi position.

48 Lift the left knee up rapidly and stretch out the arms while keeping them ready to pull back.

49 Place the foot down with a left-footed Fumikomi and an Otoshi-Uke thrust into a Kiba-Dachi position.

50 Lift the right knee up rapidly and stretch out the arms while keeping them ready to pull back.

51 Place the foot down with a right-footed Fumikomi and an Otoshi-Uke thrust into a Kiba-Dachi position.

52 Turn around on the right foot 270° pulling the left leg into the standing leg. Defensive Jodan movement with the right hand.

53 Slowly glide into the Kiba-Dachi position with a left Chudan-Zuki. The right fist is level with the chest.

54 Defend with the left hand in the Jodan region; right hand remains unchanged.

55 Glide right into a Kiba-Dachi position with a right Chudan-Zuki. As you do this, utter a long-drawn-out **Kiai**.

56 Pull the right leg into the standing leg and, as you do, lay the right hand into the open palm of the left hand.

57 Move the right leg out into the Shizentai.

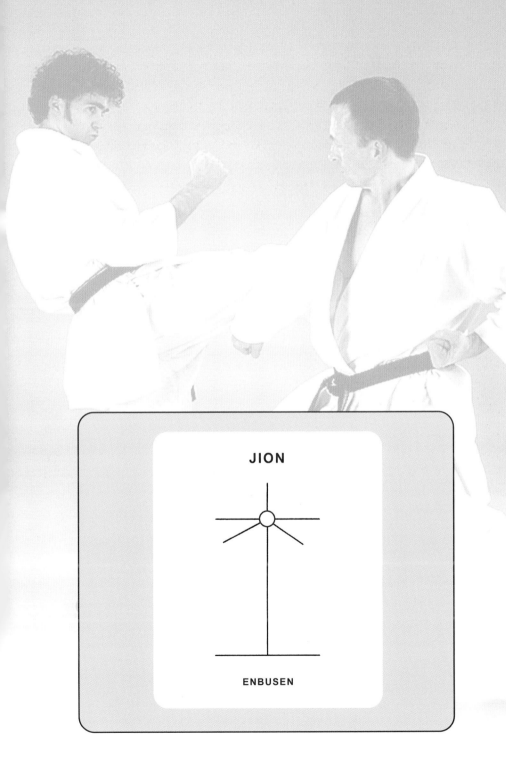

JION

ENBUSEN

Bunkai

1a

Application used for (2)-(4)

1b

1c

2a

Application used for (4)-(10)

2b

2c

2d

2e

3a

3b

Application used for (24)-(26)

3c

4a

Application used for (28)-(29)

4b

5a

Application used for (34)-(40)

5b

5c

5d

6a

Application used for (39)-(40)

6b

6c

6d

7a

7b

Application used for (45)–(46)

7c

8a

8b

Application used for (52)–(53)

4.3   Empi

Empi is the Kata for people who are fast and nimble. The rapid change in position, going deep down into the opponent, the jump and the constant switching from arm to leg techniques, which follow one directly after the other, make the Empi the most difficult Kata in the group on the way to a 1st Dan. Empi is a popular Kata that is often performed in competitions. With reference to this Kata, a Japanese Master (KANAZAWA) said: "The Empi Kata was earlier named 'Wanshu'. Its current name – 'Empi' ('flying swallow') – is derived from the fist punches to the upper region, the jump and the striking techniques as one engages the opponent and draws him on. Together, these resemble the sweeping flight – low and high – of the swallow. Similarly, the frequent switching of direction also reminds one of the changes in flight made by the swallow".

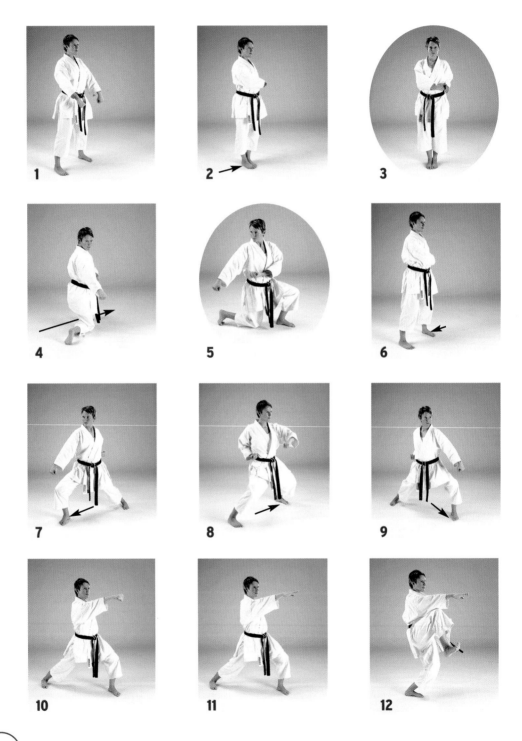

48

49

50

51

52

53

54

Sequence of actions

1   Shizentai.

2   Bring the feet together with the right coming alongside the left, while at the same time bringing the fists onto the left hip. Press the right fist into the open palm of the left hand.

3   Front view.

4   Go down onto the knee and, at an angle of 45°, execute a defensive right-handed Gedan-Barai; the left fist is held against the body at belt height in a Kamae stance.

5   Front view.

6   Stand up and place the fists over each other on the left. Right fist lies on top of the left fist.

7   Go to the right into a Zenkutsu-Dachi position with a Gedan-Barai.

8   Left foot is placed a little to the rear and into a Kiba-Dachi position; at the same time, do a left Kagi-Zuki.

9   Go forwards into the Zenkutsu-Dachi position with a left Gedan-Barai block.

10 Remain in the same position and execute a right-handed Age-Zuki strike.

11 Slowly open the right fist.

12 Execute a right-footed Hiza-Geri while the arms remain in the original position.

13 Place the foot down again well forward into a Kosa-Dachi position executing a left-handed Gedan-Zuki punch, and then defend with a right Nagashi-Uke-Jodan block.

14 Turn around 180° into a left-footed Zenkutsu-Dachi position with a right-handed Gedan-Barai to the rear; the body is leaning forward and you are looking to the rear over your shoulder.

15 Remaining in the same position, lift your upper body upright, looking forwards and executing a left Gedan-Barai.

16 Remaining standing; execute a right-handed Age-Zuki.

17 Slowly open the right fist.

18 Execute a right-footed Hiza-Geri with the arms staying in the original position.

19 Place the foot down again well forward into a Kosa-Dachi position, executing a left-handed Gedan-Zuki punch, and then defend with a right-handed Nagashi-Uke-Jodan block.

20 Turn around 180° into a left-footed Zenkutsu-Dachi position with a right-handed Gedan-Barai to the rear; the body is leaning forwards, and you are looking to the rear over your shoulder.

21 Remaining in the same position, lift your upper body upright, looking forwards and executing a left Gedan-Barai.

22 Shift your weight onto the rear leg and pull the forward leg back. Open the left hand. Look to the left.

23 Slowly bring the left leg up and, at the same time, stretch up the left hand for a Jodan-Naiwan-Uke block with the inside of the arm.

24 Place the foot down into a Kiba-Dachi position with a left arm Jodan-Naiwan-Uke.

25 Bring the right foot up quickly into the back of the left knee joint and do a Jodan-Empi with the open hand onto the right elbow, uttering a **Kiai**.

26 Front view.

27 Slowly place the right foot out into a Kiba-Dachi position and execute a left-handed Tate-Shuto-Uke. Look forwards.

28 Remaining in the same position, execute a right-handed Choku-Zuki.

29 Remaining in the same position, execute a left-handed Choku-Zuki.

30 Turn left 90° with a left-handed Gedan-Barai block into a Zenkutsu-Dachi position.

31 Remaining in the same position, execute a right-handed Age-Zuki.

32 Go forward executing a right-handed Shuto-Uke into a Kokutsu-Dachi position.

33 Bring the right foot back to the left foot.

34 Go forward executing a left-handed Shuto-Uke into a Kokutsu-Dachi position.

35 Remaining in the same position, do a right Gyaku-Zuki.

36 Go forward executing a right-handed Shuto-Uke into a Kokutsu-Dachi position.

37 Turn around 180° with a left-handed Gedan-Barai block into a Zenkutsu-Dachi position.

38 Remaining in the same position, execute a right-handed Age-Zuki.

39 Slowly open the right fist.

40 Execute a right-footed Hiza-Geri with the arms staying in the original position.

41 Place the foot down again well forward into a Kosa-Dachi position executing a left-handed Gedan-Zuki punch, and then defend with a right-handed Nagashi-Uke-Jodan block.

42 Turn around 180° into a left-footed Zenkutsu-Dachi position with a right-handed Gedan-Barai to the rear; the body is leaning forwards, and you are looking to the rear over your shoulder.

43 Remaining in the same position, lift your upper body upright, looking forwards and executing a left Gedan-Barai.

44 Standing up slowly, execute a right-handed Chudan-Teisho-Uke with the palm of the hand 90° to the right hand side. Also look right.

45 Bring the right leg up to the centre of the position, and then slowly go right 90° and execute a right-handed Teisho-Uke-Chudan block with the palm followed by a left-handed Teisho-Uke-Gedan block into a Zenkutsu-Dachi right-footed position. When moving, bring the hips round and, when doing the Teisho-Uke turn, them back again.

46 Go forward slowly into a left-footed Zenkutsu-Dachi executing a left-handed Chudan-Teisho-Uke and then a right-handed Gedan-Teisho-Uke. The hips are brought around and turned back again when executing the block.

47 Go forward slowly into a right-footed Zenkutsu-Dachi executing a right-handed Chudan-Teisho-Uke and then a left-handed Gedan-Teisho-Uke. The hips are brought around and turned back again when executing the block.

48 Change over to a Kokutsu-Dachi position with a right-handed Gedan-Barai block.

49 With a Suri-Ashi glide into a Kiba-Dachi position, defend with the left hand in the Jodan region and with the open right hand in the Chudan region.

50 Jump around 360°, pulling back for a Shuto-Uke.

51 Land in the Kokutsu-Dachi position executing a right-handed Shuto-Uke defence and uttering a **Kiai**.

52 Go backwards with a left-handed Shuto-Uke into a Kokutsu-Dachi position.

53 Bring the left leg back to the standing leg and place the fist of the right hand into the open left hand.

54 Shizentai.

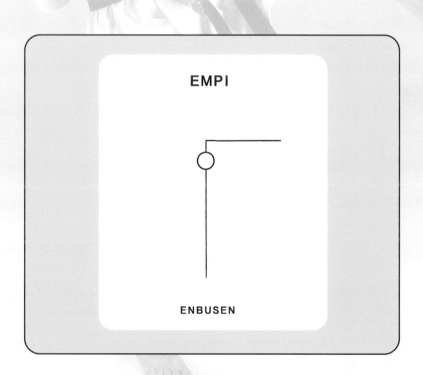

EMPI

ENBUSEN

Bunkai

1a

1b

Application used for (2)-(8)

1c

1d

1e

2a
Application used for (9)-(15)

2b

2c

2d

2e

2f

2g

3a

3b

Application used for (24)-(25)

4a

4b

Application used for (44)-(46)

4c

5a

Application used for (48)-(51)

5b

5c

4.4   Hangetsu

Hangetsu is named after the stance Hangetsu-Dachi, which is the main stance in this Kata (Hangetsu = Half-moon). It is also taught in other styles. Its earlier name was "Seishan". It is actually completely atypical for the Shotokan style, in which the Kata usually consist of explosive, rapid or powerful, dynamic movements that serve to bridge the gap during each 'chapter' of the slow passages and breathing emphases sections of the Kata. On the contrary, Hangetsu consists almost antirely of slowly executed techniques with the body completely tensed and deep breaths being taken. It is less practised in Shotokan compared to the other Kata. This is probably because Hangetsu is not typical for the Shotokan style. Nevertheless, it should be included in the basic repertoire for the 1st Dan.

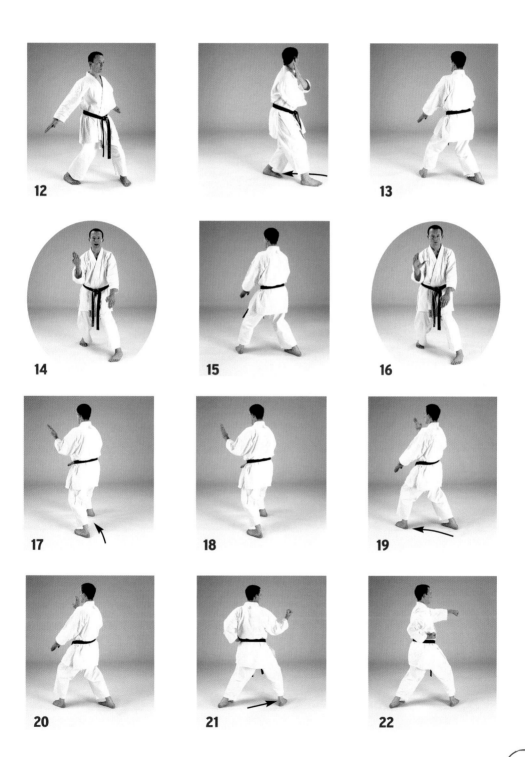

12

13

14

15

16

17

18

19

20

21

22

33

34

35

36

37

38

39

40

41

42

43

44

45

46

47

48

49

50

Sequence of actions

1   Shizentai.

2   Slowly go forward left into a Hangetsu-Dachi position executing a left Uchi-Uke.

3   Remaining in the same position, do a slow right Gyaku-Zuki.

4   Slowly go forward right into a Hangetsu-Dachi position executing a right Uchi-Uke.

5   Remaining in the same position, do a slow left Gyaku-Zuki.

6   Slowly go forward left into a Hangetsu-Dachi position executing a left Uchi-Uke.

7   Remaining in the same position, do a slow right Gyaku-Zuki.

8   Bring back both arms to the chest.

9   Stretch the arms out again slowly with an Ippon-Ken punch.

10 Remaining in the same position, slowly stretch the arms for a Yama-Kamae guard stance into the Hangetsu-Dachi position. At the same time, crossover the arms.

11 Remaining in the same position, do a Yama-Kamae guard.

12 Bring both hands slowly down to the side doing a Gedan-Morote-Shuto-Uke double-handed block.

13 Turn around 180° rapidly into a Hangetsu-Dachi position with the left leg forward and, at the same time, execute a left-handed Gedan-Shuto-Uke and a right-handed Chudan-Shuto-Uke, and utter a **Kiai**.

14 Front view.

15 Remaining in the same position, slowly execute a right-handed Tsukami-Uke defence. Turn the right lower arm slowly over and pull it in a little.

16 Front view.

17 Move forward with a right arm Gedan-Shuto-Uke and a left arm Chudan-Shuto-Uke into the Hangetsu-Dachi position.

18 Remaining in the same position, slowly execute a left-handed Tsukami-Uke defence. Turn the left lower arm slowly over and pull it in a little.

19 Move forward left with a left arm Gedan-Shuto-Uke and a right arm Chudan-Shuto-Uke into the Hangetsu-Dachi position.

20 Remaining in the same position, slowly execute a right-handed Tsukami-Uke defence. Turn the right lower arm slowly over and pull it in a little.

21 Turn right 90° executing a defensive right-handed Uchi-Uke into either a Zenkutsu-Dachi or a Hangetsu-Dachi position. (Both positions are suitable for the next nine techniques. In this book, we carry them out in the Zenkutsu-Dachi position).

22 Remaining in the same position, execute a left Gyaku-Zuki.

23 Remaining in the same position, execute a right Chudan-Zuki.

24 Turn 180° to the rear with a left Uchi-Uke.

25   Remaining in the same position, execute a right Gyaku-Zuki.

26   Remaining in the same position, execute a left Chudan-Zuki.

27   Turn right 90° executing a defensive right-handed Uchi-Uke.

28   Remaining in the same position, execute a left Gyaku-Zuki.

29   Remaining in the same position, execute a right Chudan-Zuki.

30   Slowly lift the left leg up and pull the arm up for a vertical Tate-Uraken punch.

31   Slowly turn 180° to the rear and place the foot down in a Kokutsu-Dachi position with a left Tate-Uraken.

32   Pull the rear leg forwards past the other.

33   Execute a left-footed Mae-Geri.

34   Place the foot down into a Zenkustu-Dachi position with a left Gedan-Barai.

35   Remaining in the same position, execute a right Gyaku-Zuki.

36   Remaining in the same position, execute a left Age-Uke block.

37   Slowly lift the right leg up and pull the arm up for a vertical Tate-Uraken punch.

38   Slowly turn 180° to the rear and place the foot down in a Kokutsu-Dachi position with a right Tate-Uraken.

39   Pull the rear leg forwards past the other.

40   Execute a right-footed Mae-Geri.

41   Place the foot down into a Zenkustu-Dachi position with a right Gedan-Barai.

42   Remaining in the same position, execute a left Gyaku-Zuki.

43   Remaining in the same position, execute a right Age-Uke block.

44   Slowly lift the left leg up and pull the arm up for a vertical Tate-Uraken punch.

45   Slowly turn 180° to the rear and place the foot down in a Kokutsu-Dachi position with a left Tate-Uraken.

46   Using the right leg, execute a Mikazuki-Geri circular kick into the open hand of the outstretched left arm.

47   Place the right foot down to the rear into a left-footed Zenkustu-Dachi position with a right Gyaku-Zuki Gedan, uttering a **Kiai**.

48   Pull the forward leg back into a Neko-Ashi-Dachi cat stance, bringing the fists down to the hips.

49   Remaining in the same position, slowly execute a Gedan-Morote-Teisho-Uke.

50   Bring the forward leg back into the Shizentai position.

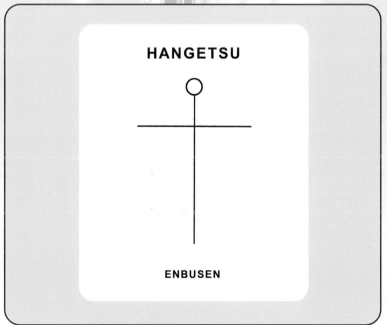

HANGETSU

ENBUSEN

Bunkai

1a

Application used for (10)-(13)

1b

1c

1d

1e

2a **2b**

Application used for (14)-(15)

3a **3b**

Application used for (30)-(36)

3c **3d**

3e

3f

4.5 Kanku-Dai

Kanku-Dai, which is known as "Kushanku" in other styles, consists of numerous elements from all of the Heian Kata combined with some new aspects. Its name means "to look at the sky", which is derived from its first movement. It is one of the longest Kata in Shotokan, and legend has it that it was taught in China starting in the time of the Ming Dynasty.

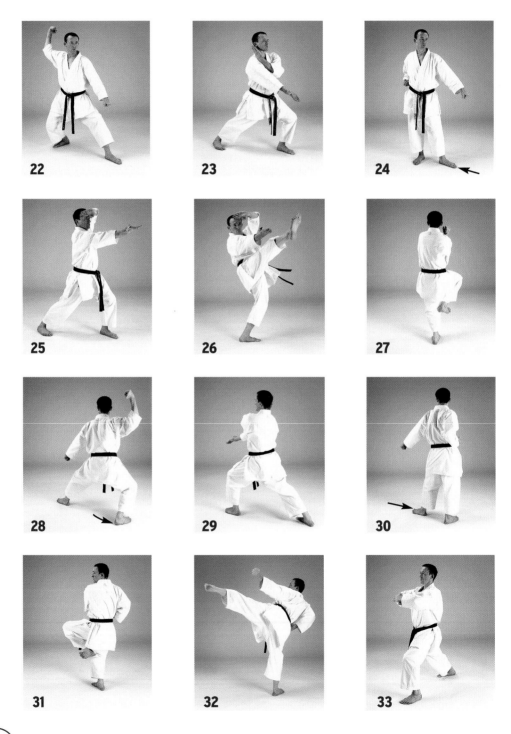

53

54

55

56

57

58

59

60

72

73

74

75

76

77

78

Sequence of actions

1 Shizentai.

2 Slowly position the fingertips and thumbs together.

3 Slowly lift the arms with your gaze following their movement.

4 Quickly spread the arms outwards and, when they are at right-angles to the shoulders, stop abruptly.

5 Then bring them down and lay the right hand in the left one.

6 Go left 90° into a Kokutsu-Dachi position executing a left-handed Jodan-Haishu-Uke.

7 Go right into a Kokutsu-Dachi position executing a right-handed Jodan-Haishu-Uke.

8 Slowly stand up into a Hachi-Dachi start position executing a left-handed Tate-Shuto-Uke.

9 Execute a right-fisted Choku-Zuki punch.

10 Using the same arm, defend with a Uchi-Uke turning the hips in.

11 Execute a left-fisted Choku-Zuki punch.

12 Using the same arm, defend with a Uchi-Uke turning the hips in.

13 Bring the left leg in a little closer. Fists are laid one on top of the other on the left hip.

14 Execute a rising sidekick Yoko-Geri-Keage with the right leg to the rear and, at the same time, a right-fisted Uraken-Uchi.

15 Place the foot down into a Kokutsu-Dachi position with a left-handed Shuto-Uke.

16 Go forward into a Kokutsu-Dachi position with a right-handed Shuto-Uke.

17 Go forward into a Kokutsu-Dachi position with a left-handed Shuto-Uke.

18 Go forward into a Zenkutsu-Dachi position with a right-handed Nukite stab, and utter a **Kiai**.

19 Turn around rearwards 180° with a left Age-Shuto-Uke and a right Shuto-Uchi.

20 Mae-Geri kick with the right leg; arms remain unchanged.

21 Turn around rearwards 180° and pull back for a Manji-Uke into a Kokutsu-Dachi position.

22 Place the foot down again with a Manji-Uke into a left-footed Kokutsu-Dachi position.

23 Execute a right Gedan-Nukite and, at the same time, do a left Jodan-Te-Nagashi-Uke into a left-footed Zenkutsu-Dachi position.

24 Slowly pull the left leg backwards into an 'L'-shaped Renoji-Dachi position with a left Gedan-Barai.

25 Go forward with a left Age-Shuto-Uke and a right Shuto-Uchi in the Zenkutsu-Dachi position.

26 Mae-Geri kick with the right leg; arms remain unchanged.

27 Turn around rearwards 180° and pull back for a Manji-Uke into a Kokutsu-Dachi position.

28 Place the foot down again with a Manji-Uke into a left-footed Kokutsu-Dachi position.

29 Execute a right Gedan-Nukite and, at the same time, do a left Jodan-Te-Nagashi-Uke into a left-footed Zenkutsu-Dachi position.

30 Slowly pull the left leg backwards into an 'L'-shaped Renoji-Dachi position with a left Gedan-Barai.

31 Lay the fists one over the other on the right hip and, at the same time, lift the left knee up. Look left.

32 Execute a rising sidekick Yoko-Geri-Keage with the left leg to the side and, at the same time, a Uraken-Uchi.

33 Place the leg down into a Zenkutsu-Dachi position with a right Mae-Empi into the open hand.

34 Bring the right leg in. Fists are laid one on the other on the left hip.

35 Execute a rising sidekick Yoko-Geri-Keage to the right and, at the same time, a Uraken.

36 Place the leg down into a Zenkutsu-Dachi position with a left Mae-Empi into the open hand.

37 Turn around left 180° with a left Shuto-Uke into a Kokutsu-Dachi position.

38 Go forward 45° to the right with a right Shuto-Uke into a Kokutsu-Dachi position.

39 Go forward 135° to the right with a right Shuto-Uke into a Kokutsu-Dachi position.

40 Go forward 45° to the left with a Shuto-Uke into a Kokutsu-Dachi position.

41 Place the left leg out at 45° and, at the same time, execute a left Age-Shuto-Uke and a right Jodan-Shuto-Uke into a Zenkutsu-Dachi position.

42 Mae-Geri kick with the right leg; arms remain unchanged.

43 Snap the right leg back, moving for a Uraken-Uchi.

44 Go well forward into a Kosa-Dachi position with a right Tate-Uraken-Uchi.

45 Place the right leg back again with a right Uchi-Uke.

46 Remaining in the same position, execute a left Gyaku-Zuki.

47 Remaining in the same position, execute a right Chudan-Zuki.

48 Turn around 180° to the rear with an Oi-Komi Ura Zuki, lifting the right knee up rapidly.

49 Place the foot down on the ground, balancing and resting on the hands while holding the left leg stretched-out to the rear.

50 Turn around 180° with a left Gedan-Shuto-Uke into a deep Kokutsu-Dachi position.

51 Side view.

52 Go forward with a right Shuto-Uke.

53 Turn on the standing leg 270° with a left Uchi-Uke into a Zenkutsu-Dachi position.

54 Remaining in the same position, execute a right-handed Gyaku-Zuki.

55 Turn around 180° with a right Uchi-Uke into a Zenkutsu-Dachi position.

56 Remaining in the same position, execute a left Gyaku-Zuki.

57 Remaining in the same position, execute a right Chudan-Zuki.

58 Bring the left leg in a little closer. Fists are laid one on top of the other on the left hip.

59 Execute a rising sidekick Yoko-Geri to the right and, at the same time, a Uraken.

60 Place the foot down into a Kokutsu-Dachi position with a left-handed Shuto-Uke.

61 Go forward with a right Nukite into a Zenkutsu-Dachi position.

62 Turn in on the right foot and bring the palm of the stabbing Nukite hand up to the ear.

63 Turn around 180° on the right foot, then place the foot down with a left Tate-Uraken into a Kiba-Dachi position.

64 Slip to the left with a Suri-Ashi and with a left Tettsui-Uchi into a Kiba-Dachi position.

65 Remaining in the same position, put the right elbow into the left hand.

66 Remaining in the same position, look right and place the fists one on top of the other on the left hip.

67 Remaining in the same position, execute a right Gedan Barai.

68 Turn around on the right leg 180° with a left Mikazuki-Geri. Raise the left arm rapidly up and hold the right arm in the Gedan position.

69 Place the foot down with a Fumikomi into the Kiba-Dachi position and, at the same time, execute a left Gedan Kake-Uke and a right Jodan Kamae position.

70 Execute a right Gedan Otoshi-Zuki into the Kiba-Dachi position.

71 Stand upright with a Jodan Juji-Uke into the Hachi-Dachi position

72 Slowly turn around 270° on the right leg into a right-footed Zenkutsu-Dachi position bringing the arms in a slow Juji-Kamae onto the chest and closing the hands.

73 Execute a Mae Tobi-Geri kick, uttering a **Kiai** and, at the same time, moving to do a Uraken.

74 Place the foot down with a right Tate-Uraken-Uchi in the Zenkutsu-Dachi position.

75 Turn 180° on the right foot and pull back for a right Gedan-Sukui-Uke.

76 Execute a right Gedan Sukui-Uke in the Kiba-Dachi position.

77 Bring the arms up and stand up in the Hachi-Dachi position.

78 Shizentai.

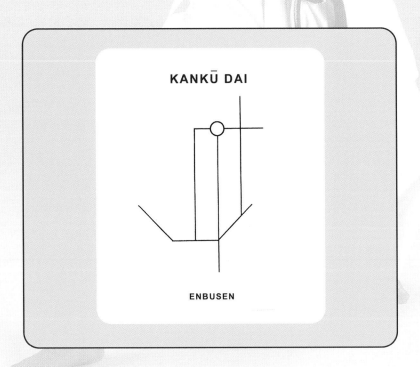

KANKŪ DAI

ENBUSEN

Bunkai

1a

Application used for (6)

2a

2b

Application used for (34)-(36)

2c

3a

Application used for (48)-(52)

3b

3c

3d

3e

4a

4b

Application used for (67)-(70)

4c

4d

5a

5b

Application used for (71)-(72)

5   **KARATE STANCES**

5   Karate Stances

The Kata include all the Karate stance positions. They make it possible to fight from short, middle and long distances. Therefore, at this juncture, here is a short set of illustrations depicting the Karate stance positions.

5.1 Heisoku-Dachi

5.2 Musubi-Dachi

5.3 Heiko-Dachi

5.4 Hachiji-Dachi

5.5   Zenkutsu-Dachi

5.6 Kokutsu-Dachi

5.7 Kiba-Dachi

5.8 Neko-Achi-Dachi

5.9 Sanchin-Dachi

5.10 Fudo-Dachi

5.11 Kosa-Dachi

5.12   Renoji-Dachi

6 RECURRING TECHNIQUES IN THE KATA

6.1 Manji-Uke

At this point we have the opportunity to have a look at some of the recurring techniques that often appear in the Shotokan Kata – by phases and in detail. It is worth paying attention to the starting position, the movement(s) in between and the correct final position of these techniques. These should be practised intensively in order to avoid mistakes.

6.2   Yoko-Geri, Uraken, Empi

6.3 Kakiwake-Uke

1

2

3

6.4 Tate-Shuto-Uke

1

2

6.5 Haishu-Uke

1

2

3

6.6 Morote-Uke

1

2

6.7 Fumikomi

1

2

Notes to the Kata descriptions:

Each Kata begins and ends with a bow – the Rei. The heels are close together during this movement. Then one adopts the natural Shizentai position in Hachi-Dachi. At the same time as the right leg comes into this position, the arms are crossed over in a short defensive movement. In the Yoi position, the arms are held directly in front of the thighs.

The fist techniques Oi-Zuki and Gyaku-Zuki are generally carried out at the Chudan region height in the Kata. If a different height is required (Gedan or Jodan), then this is also indicated in the texts.

Side or front views are shown in the Kata sequences in the oval illustrations for the purpose of clarity.

7 Appendix

7.1 Bibliography

Enoeda, K.: *Shotokan Karate Advanced Kata Vol. 1-3*. Norwich 1983-86.

Enoeda, K.: *Shotokan Karate 10th Kyu to 6th Kyu*. London 1996.

Enoeda, K.: *Shotokan Karate 5th Kyu to Black Belt*. London 1996.

Funakoshi, G.: *Karate-do Kyohan*. Tokyo 1978.

Funakoshi, G.: *Karate-do: Mein Weg*. Weidental 1983.

Grupp, J.: *Shotokan Karate. Technik, Training, Prüfung*. Aachen 2000.

Gursharan, S.: *Advanced Shotokan Karate Handbook*. Bedford 1997.

Hassell, R.G.: *Gespräche mit dem Meister Masatoshi Nakayama*. Lauda 1999.

Hassell, R.G.: *Shotokan Karate: Its History and Evolution*. St. Louis 1998.

Healy, K.: *A step-by-step guide to Shotokan Karate*. London 2000.

Kanazawa, H.: *Shotokan Karate Kata Band 1-2*. Tokyo 1982.

Milon, M.: *Apprenez vos Katas de Base du Karaté Shotokan*. Paris 1997.

Nakayama, M.: *Karate-Do. Dynamic Karate*. Sprendlingen 1972.

Nakayama, M.: *Karate perfekt. Band 5-8*. Niedernhausen 1989.

Nakayama, M.: *Best Karate. Band 9-11*. Tokyo, New York, London 1989.

Pflüger, A., *Karate 1 und Karate 2*. Niedernhausen 1999 and 1987.

Reilly, R.L.: *Complete Shotokan Karate*. Boston 1998.

Reilly, R.L.: *The Secrets of Shotokan Karate*. Boston 2000.

Schlatt: *Shotokan No Hyakkajiten*. Lauda 1995.

Schmesser, E.: *Bunkai. Secrets of Karate Kata, Volume 1*: The Tekki Series. Missouri 2000.

Trimble, A./Morris, V.: *Karate Kata Applications*. London 1995.

Tartaglia, F.: *Shotokan-Kata bis zum Schwarzgurt*. Göppingen 2000.

V. Weenen, J.: *Advanced Shotokan Karate Kata*. Wollaston 1987.

7.2 Glossary

Japanese Technical Terms

A

Age-Uke	A rising defensive block
Antei	Balance, equilibrium
Ashi-Barai	Leg sweep attack
Atemi-points	Vital points on the body
Awasete	. . . equals . . .

B

Barai	Sweeping movement
Bunkai	Demonstrating techniques of a Kata with a partner
Budo	Japanese martial arts in general

C

Choku-Zuki	A straight punch from the Hachi-Dachi
Chudan	Mid-section of the body, chest height

D

Dachi	Stance, position
Dai	Big, great
Dan	Black belt grade, grade of master
De-Ai	A counterattack while at the same time defending successfully
Do	The path to spiritual and good moral behaviour
Dojo	The training hall

E

Embusen	Diagram of the steps for a Kata
Empi	Elbow
Empi-Uchi	An attack delivered with the elbow

F

Fudo	Firm, deeply rooted
Fumi	Stamping movement with the foot
Fumikomi-Achi	A step made with a stamping movement

G

Gaiwan	Outer edge of the arm
Gedan	Lower area of the body, below the belt area
Gedan-Barai	Blocking an attack with a downwards movement
Gohon-Kumite	Five-step prearranged sparring
Gyaku	Reverse side of the front leg
Gyaku-Zuki	Reverse punch (e.g., left foot forward, right Zuki)

H

Haito	The (sword) edge of the hand
Haiwan	The upper edge of the arm
Hajime	"Begin!" The command given for opponents to start a contest
Hangetsu-Dachi	'Half-moon' or crescent posture
Hanmi	Stance with the hips half-turned to one side
Hara	'Belly', centre of the body, the body's spiritual and inner centre of gravity
Heisoku-Dachi	Standing posture, feet joined together
Hidari	Left
Hikite	Series of movements conducted as a technique as the arm is pulled backwards
Hiza	Knee

I

Ippon	A full point
Ippon-Kumite	An attack using only one technique (step)

J

Jogai	Outside the limits of the mat contest area
Jiyu	Freestyle
Jiyu-Kumite	Freestyle fighting
Jiyu-Ippon-Kumite	Freestyle one-step sparring
Jodan	Upper level (Head and neck height)
Juji-Uke	Cross hands, wrists block

K

Kachi	Contest winner
Kaeshi-Ippon-Kumite	Sequence with reverse one-step attack
Kai-Ashi	Step
Kakato	Heel
Kamae	Starting position, guard

Karateka	Anyone who practises Karate
Karate-Gi	Karate training uniform, dress
Kata	Form, sequence
Keage	Kick with a withdrawing whipping action
Kekomi	A penetrating kick
Keri	Kick (also spelled Geri)
Kiai	Karate shout
Kiba-Dachi	Sideways posture, legs apart
Kihon	A basic movement, technique
Kime	Focussing all one's physical and psychological force (at the end of the technique)
Kizami-Zuki	A punch with the forward arm
Kokutsu-Dachi	Upright stance leaning back on the rear leg
Kumite	Sparring with a partner

M

Mae	Front, in front
Mae-Ashi-Geri	A front kick with the leading leg
Mae-Empi	front attack with the elbow held level
Mae-Geri	A kick to the front with the rear leg
Makiwara	Woven raffia tied to a post for punch training
Mawashi-Geri	A roundhouse kick (mawashi – 'in a circle')
Mawate	Turn
Migi	Right, on the right, right-hand side
Mikazuki-Geri	A crescent kick tracing an arc of a circle
Mokuso	A meditative posture for concentrating and breathing with closed eyes
Morote-Uchi-Ude-Uke	Defence of the middle area using locked hands from the inside
Musubi-Dachi	Feet positioned at 60° apart, heels touching together

N

Nagashi-Uke	Defensive block using the inside of the forearm
Naiwan	Inside of the arm
Neko-Ashi-Dachi	'Cat stance', the weight of the body is almost completely over the rear leg
Nukite	Stabbing blow (the hand is held vertically to the ground)

O

Oi-Zuki	Straight fist punch, lunge punch
Otoshi-Uke	Defence from above downwards

R

Randori	Free-fighting
Rei	Karate bow, greeting
Ren-Geri	Two-step kicking movement
Ren-Zuki	Alternate punches

S

Sabaki	Dodging movement (also Tai-Sabaki)
Sanbon-Kumite	Three-step sparring
Sanbon-Zuki	Alternate punches in threes
Sanchin-Dachi	Standing stance with knees and feet turned in to protect the lower abdomen
Seiza	Kneeling posture sitting on the heels at the beginning and end of training
Sensei-Ni-Rei	Formal bow of greeting to training teacher
Shiai	Competition
Shitei Kata	Compulsory Kata
Shizentai	Natural basic posture with the feet shoulder-width apart
Shomen	Centred to the front
Shuto-Uchi	Direct attack with the 'sword-hand', edge of the hand
Shuto-Uke	Defensive movement with edge of the hand
Shuwan	Underside of the arm
Sochin-Dachi	Position in the Kata Sochin (alternative name is Fudo-Dachi)
Soto-Uke	Defensive block using the outer edge of the forearm from the inside to the outside
Suri-Ashi	Sliding step (starting with the front foot)

T

Tate-Empi	A rising elbow blow
Tate-Shuto-Uke	Blocking a blow using the edge of the stretched-out hand
Tate-Uraken-Uchi	Defence using the back of the hand held vertically
Tate-Zuki	A punch delivered with the fist, palm along a vertical plane
Te	Hand
Teisho	Base of the palm of the hand
Teisho-Uke	Block with palm of the hand
Te-Otoshi-Uke	Hand block from above downwards; the palm of the hand is parallel to the ground

Tokui Kata	'Favourite' Kata
Tori	The attacker
Tsugi-Ashi	Sliding the feet forwards one after the other, rear foot first
Tsuki	Blow, punch (also spelled Zuki)

U

Uchi	Strike
Uchi-Ude-Uke	Inside arm block of the middle zone
Ude	Forearm
Uke	A defensive movement
Uraken-Uchi	Strike with the back of the fist
Ura-Mawashi-Geri	Roundhouse with the heel or sole of the foot
Ushiro-Geri	A back kick

W

Waza	Technique
Wazari	A half-point

Y

Yame	Stop!
Yoi	"Get ready!" (This command is used to signal the adoption of the Shizentai starting posture
Yoko	Lateral, side
Yoko-Geri	Sidekick
Yoko-Uraken-Uchi	Sideways strike with the back of the hand
Yori-Ashi	Sideways sliding movement

Z

Zanshin	Vigilance, constant concentration
Zenkutsu-Dachi	Position with weight on forward leg
Zuki	Blow, punch (also spelled Tsuki)

7.3 Acknowledgements

I would like to thank Tanja Schwabe, Felix Engeln, Angelo Carnarius and John Dahl for posing for the actions. Thanks go also to Benedikt Sommer and Tanja Schwabe for their encouragement in assisting with the content, Gerhard Axmann for his work on the cover picture as well as Jana Rohleder and Christian Fritsch for the photos in the book. In addition I would like to thank the Kamikaze Company and, particularly Markus Hinschberger for their support.

Contact the Author
Questions about the book or queries about courses
can be sent to the author at joachimgrupp@web.de.

A Note of Warning

"By nature, the techniques described in this book and all other techniques used in fighting sports are dangerous. It is advised that training this fighting sport is only undertaken under the supervision and direction of an expert. Please be careful when training in the techniques described in this book. Neither the author nor the pblisher can be held responsible for damages brought about by one's own carelessness. Also, please observe the legal provisions in your own country."

Photo & Illustration Credits

Cover Photo, Photos: Christian and Roland Fritsch, Fotostudio
                         FTB – Werbefotografie, Berlin, Germany

Cover Design: Sabine Groten, Germany

Joachim Grupp
Shotokan Karate Kumite

Following on from KIHON and KATA, this fourth book in the series covers the third pillar of Shotokan Karate – KUMITE – meaning sparring. Using numerous photos, the Kareteka is lead, step-by-step, through the techniques. Tips on self-defense apart from the competitive aspects round off the subject.

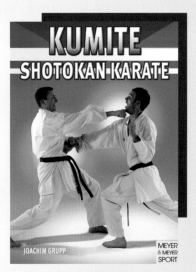

168 pages, full-color print
509 photos, 11 illustrations
Paperback, 6¹/₂" x 9¹/₄"
ISBN: 978-1-84126-151-5
$ 17.95 US/$ 29.95 AUS
£ 12.95 UK/€ 16.90

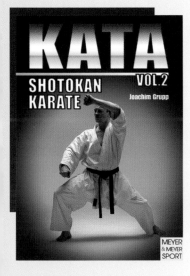

Joachim Grupp
Shotokan Karate KATA Vol.2

The Master Kata described in this book belong to the advanced part of the repertoire and carry on from the Kata introduced in Volume 1. This then completes the list of all the Shotokan Karate Kata. There are 9 Kata with Bunkai in this book: Sochin, Meikyo, Chinte, Kanku-Sho, Wankan, Ji'in, Jitte, Gankaku, Unsu. There are more than 600 photos and detailed descriptions, which allow a deeper understanding of the Kata and their application.

152 pages, Two-color print, 682 photos
Paperback, 5³/₄" x 8¹/₄"
ISBN: 978-1-84126-091-4
$ 17.95 US/$ 29.95 AUS
£ 12.95 UK/€ 16.90

The Sports Publisher

MEYER
& MEYER
SPORT
25 YEARS

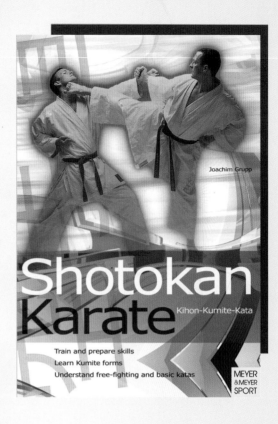